The Swedish Atheist, the Scuba Diver and Other Apologetic Rabbit Trails

RANDAL RAUSER

IVP Books

An imprint of InterVarsity Press
Downers Grove, Illinois

InterVarsity Press
P.O. Box 1400, Downers Grove, IL 60515-1426
World Wide Web: www.ivpress.com
E-mail: email@ivpress.com

*InterVarsity Press® is the book-publishing division of InterVarsity Christian Fellowship/USA®, a
movement of students and faculty active on campus at hundreds of universities, colleges and schools
of nursing in the United States of America, and a member movement of the International Fellowship
of Evangelical Students. For information about local and regional activities, write Public Relations
Dept., InterVarsity Christian Fellowship/USA, 6400 Schroeder Rd., P.O. Box 7895, Madison, WI
53707-7895, or visit the IVCF website at <www.intervarsity.org>.*

*Published in association with the Books & Such Literary Agency, Janet Kobobel Grant, 52 Mission
Circle, Suite 122, PMB 170, Santa Rosa, CA 95409-5370, www.booksandsuch.biz.*

All Scripture quotations, unless otherwise indicated, are taken from the Holy Bible, New
International Version®. NIV®. *Copyright ©1973, 1978, 1984 by International Bible Society. Used
by permission of Zondervan Publishing House. All rights reserved.*

Cover design: Cindy Kiple
Images: diving helmet: © Laurent Nicod/iStockphoto
  man with tea: © knape/iStockphoto
Interior design: Beth Hagenberg

ISBN 978-0-8308-3778-6

Printed in the United States of America ∞

Library of Congress Cataloging-in-Publication Data

Rauser, Randal D.
 The Swedish atheist, the scuba diver, and other apologetic rabbit trails
/ Randal Rauser.
    p. cm.
 Includes bibliographical references.
 ISBN 978-0-8308-3778-6 (pbk. : alk. paper)
 1. Apologetics. I. Title.
 BT1103.R38 2012
 239—dc23

                                                                                    2012027674

P	18	17	16	15	14	13	12	11	10	9	8	7	6	5	4	3	2	1
Y	27	26	25	24	23	22	21	20	19	18	17	16	15	14	13	12

This book is dedicated to you, Reader.
Thanks for being there!

God breathes through us so completely . . .
so gently we hardly feel it . . .
yet, it is our everything.
Thank you God.

John Coltrane

Contents

Introduction

★ ★ ★

Since this is a book about apologetics, it makes sense to begin with a description of what I take apologetics to be. Open a dictionary and you'll find a definition like this:

> a·pol·o·get·ics *n.* The branch of theology that defends Christian belief and critiques opposing belief systems.

That's more or less correct. However, we all operate with our own subtle understandings of words that go beyond dictionary denotations. For years my understanding of apologetics was a good deal more militaristic than that offered by Webster's. Had I ever bothered to write it down, it might have looked like this:

> a·pol·o·get·ics *n.* Christian intellectual warfare with non-Christian belief systems that utilizes the weaponry of sound argumentation.

If you're wondering why I held such a battle-happy view of apologetics, let me assure you that the warfare motif hardly originated with me. Many Christians trace the conception of apologetics as battle right back to the New Testament. After all, Paul describes the Christian life in terms of wearing armor and wielding a sword (Ephesians 6:10-18). What's more, he bequeaths to apologists a mandate that, but for a few words, could have been excerpted from a William Wallace speech: "We demolish arguments and every pretension that sets itself up against the knowledge of God, and we take captive every thought to make it obedient to Christ" (2 Corinthians 10:5). Terms like "demolishing" and "taking captive" certainly sound like warfare, so it doesn't take much imagination to picture the apologist as beating back the forces of darkness with arguments and evidence.

However, as solid as apologetics' militaristic credentials may seem, I was eventually forced to confront two serious shortcomings with this view. First, thinking of apologetics in terms of warfare tends to create highly adversarial situations in which the apologist is pitted against an "enemy." The result is a polarizing framework of "I'm right and you're wrong" that blurs the fact that nobody is right—or wrong—all the time. You've probably heard it said that truth is the first casualty of war. The subtle distinctions of real life have no place in war, which divides the world into a simple binary between good guys and bad guys. The same thing happens when the war is shifted to the apologetic battlefield. When we practice warfare-based apologetics, we tend to miss the right, good and true in the "enemy," as well as the wrong, bad and false in ourselves.[1]

Second, and most disturbingly, I discovered that the warfare approach to apologetics produced almost no change in others. Even when I "demolished" other people's arguments (or at least thought I had), they typically didn't see it that way. More often than not they'd continue to crouch in the ruins of their worldview, firing RPGs back at my rumbling convoy of apologetic Humvees like stubborn insurgents.

It didn't take much of that before I started to ask myself, what good is winning arguments if I lose people? And that led to the recognition (for me a minor revolution at the time) that the warfare motif was missing something. Maybe apologetics should be concerned with more than defeating arguments. Maybe it should also be concerned with persuading people. And while warfare can compel, it rarely persuades.

Scripture itself supports the notion that persuasion is central to apologetics. Although the militaristic motifs are present in the New Testament, for the early Christians the goal of persuasion was always primary. "When Silas and Timothy came from Macedonia, Paul devoted himself exclusively to preaching, testifying to the Jews that Jesus was the Christ" (Acts 18:5). Paul didn't spend time testifying to the messiahship of Jesus so he could win arguments. Rather, his goal was to win people through arguments: "Every Sabbath he reasoned in the synagogue, trying to persuade Jews and Greeks" (Acts 18:4).

So with the military motif of apologetics in my rearview mirror, what was my new definition? Something like this:

a·pol·o·get·ics *n*. The discipline of making converts to Christianity through the use of argument and evidence.

This made more sense. After all, Jesus commanded us to go into the world to make disciples, not simply win arguments. And so I began to pursue apologetics as a grand project focused on converting people to my Christian beliefs. That meant honing my arguments and delivery to facilitate the prized conversion of my unsuspecting future convert—a person formerly known as the enemy.

Unfortunately it wasn't long before storm clouds appeared once again. I began to notice that most of the non-Christians with whom I interacted viewed apologetics with derision and suspicion. It soon became clear to me that the derision was directed largely at the evangelistic emphasis of my apologetics.

Why? Well, have you ever have a friend who joined Amway? An innocent invitation to go out for coffee soon becomes an invitation to "join the Amway family." That's the way people look at

Christian apologists. The secret is out: apologists use arguments so they can make converts. It doesn't take long for would-be converts to notice that an apologist wants to talk with them only in order to convert them.

In other words, real conversation is not possible. Would a politician admit that his opponent holds a superior economic policy? Would a lawyer confess her client's guilt? Would a salesperson advise against the purchase of his company's inferior products? So why would anyone trust an apologist whose raison d'être is simply to make converts?

These troubling reflections led me to a third revolution in my definition of apologetics. I didn't reject rigorous argumentation or evangelistic persuasion—far from it. Yet while I continued to embrace both tactics, I came to recognize that they must be submitted to another end: the pursuit of truth.

In his famous exchange with Pilate, Jesus Christ declared, "For this reason I was born, and for this I came into the world, to testify to the truth" (John 18:37). If Jesus came to testify to the truth, then surely truth should be at the center of our concerns as well. What good is it to win an argument or a convert if your position is not true? If Jesus was shaped by the truth so completely that he could be equated with truth (see John 14:6), then surely Christ-followers ought likewise to seek to be shaped by the truth.

With that in mind, I gradually came to realize that the best apologetic witness is found when we subordinate all other goals to the tireless pursuit of the truth. When people see that you can be trusted to seek the truth above all else, they start to listen—and you start to listen to them, too!

That led me to the definition of apologetics I now embrace:

a·pol·o·ge·tics *n*. The rigorous pursuit of truth in conversation.

*   *   *

I once thought the perfect setting for an apologetic exchange was the lecture hall, where two individuals engaged in a knock-down, drag-out debate in front of a rapt audience. But that reeks of combat. Let's get rid of the polarized audience and constricting debate resolution—and definitely throw out the timer!

Some conversations are meant to be savored as part of what I call the "grande conversation." Grande conversation takes hours or even weeks—however long the people talking want to spend—and participants pursue a rigorous, trusting, honest sharing of ideas in a comfortable, noncombative environment. (Why not simply the "grand" conversation? Because the word "grand" ain't itself sufficiently grand to do the job. But adding an "e" gives it a much-needed touch of gravitas, don't you think?)

So this is where we find ourselves now. I love apologetics and think it worth a lifetime of study and reflection. But I don't primarily see apologetics as the winning of arguments or converts. Rather, apologetics is the discovery of truth through a winding, weaving, honest, aimless, pointless and completely purposeful conversation in which two or more people desperately want to understand the way things really are.

That simple yet stunning idea—that people of goodwill can seek and find truth—is the topic of this book.

1

The Sacramental Properties
of Caffeine

* * *

So. Where should we pursue our grande conversation? I can already hear those of you clamoring to "take it to the pub! Preferably a 'locals only' establishment that sells the best regional microbrew." That's a fair suggestion, but I'm going to propose that we bypass licensed establishments. During our grande conversation we'll need to keep our razor-sharp analytic wits about us, and drinking depressants by the pint is probably not the best way to do that.

I hear you back-to-nature types suggesting a park bench. After all, Jesus preached on mounts and plains, so why not a dialogue in a lovely natural setting? It's an admirable sentiment to be sure, but the comfort level of park benches drops sharply during extended conversations—to say nothing of the abiding threat of mosquitoes and pigeon droppings.

Instead, I suggest a coffee shop. The invigorating effects of caffeine are well-known (although be forewarned that if you're dialoguing with a Mormon, he or she will be limited to fruit juice or herbal tea). What's more, these days coffee shops are recognized as the happening places for deep discussion. Certainly that's the easier part of the decision.

But now we have to decide which coffee shop. Since I'm an upwardly mobile fellow, you might think that I'd elect for a visit to an outlet of that colossal caffeinated corporation Starbucks. In some respects that's not a bad idea. Starbucks has reasonably good coffee, and it does offer a clean and sterile environment (although, to be fair, so does a hospital). As an added bonus, setting our grande conversation in Starbucks offers the potential of lucrative product placement. Surely Howard Schultz would jump at the chance to get his company's product plugged in an apologetics book—Christians, after all, buy a lot of coffee. And I could be so subtle writing in the adverts that you'd never even notice. Witness: "Great point, Mr. Atheist. Before I respond, let me just take another sip of my delicious Caramel Frappuccino.®"

While it's a tempting thought, I just can't bring myself to sell out to filthy lucre. Whether I like it or not, the fact is that good old SBUX is just not the preferred venue for a grande conversation. The main problem (barring the fact that I don't care for the color green) is that Starbucks tends to offer a rushed environment with a steady stream of soccer moms and real estate agents lining up to grab their Frappuccinos and Americanos before they continue on with the business of the day. Even more distracting is the bonds trader who cannot stop jabbering into his Bluetooth long enough to make eye contact with the barista taking his order.

For our exercise we'll cast our gaze toward the local university, homing in on one of those trendy bordering neighborhoods with an endearing bohemian flavor, tree-lined streets, used-book shops and dilapidated frat houses. There we are sure to find a flavorful independent coffee shop where words like *organic* and *fair-trade* are not just part of a corporate advertising campaign and where they expect you to stay for an extended period of time.

Come to think of it, I know the perfect place: the Beatnik Bean. It has all the essentials for the most highfalutin grande conversation. Let me give you a quick rundown of the main characteristics of a great "grande conversation" coffee shop so you know what to look for in your neighborhood:

- rustic furniture with a "garage sale meets *Antiques Roadshow*" appeal (you'll be wondering, is this thing I'm sitting on a piece of junk or a lost treasure from the palace of the Sun King?)
- lilting jazz music, seventies MOR, reggae or a mix thereof
- garish local art hung on the walls (for sale, of course—as if anybody would actually buy it)
- loads of scruffy students intently cramming for finals
- the aroma of freshly baked muffins and strong, smoky espresso
- amiable baristas with dreadlocks, nose rings and unusual ethnic names like Ashank, Nadia and Chiba

Put those elements together and you have all the pieces in place for a grande conversation to remember. So what are we waiting for? Let's go!

That's right, let's go. That means you, too, dear Reader. You're not going to be sitting in the bleachers as a mere spectator in my book.

If you're wondering how you, the reader of this book, can be part of the grande conversation, think about avatars. In the pages to come, I'd like you to adopt your own avatar and enter into the virtual world of the Beatnik Bean. As for your identity, I've tried to keep that wide open by writing you in as a silent, faceless individual named, rather unimaginatively, "Reader."

This isn't as bad as it sounds because in this story you can imagine yourself to look and act any way you like, as long as it doesn't impinge on the narrative. (For example, please don't make yourself into a hundred-foot giant because you'll never fit in the chair next to me—and you'll probably make me spill my coffee, too.) As for appearance, come as you are. Unlike some virtual realities, our little coffee shop isn't an escape from reality.

Rather, the following pages are a journey into the heart of truth.

The Hidden Chapter Without a Name

(a.k.a. the Chapter Between Chapters 1 and 2)

When I was growing up, I loved discovering an album with a hidden track not listed on the record sleeve. There was an air of mystery and added value when I discovered that I'd paid for ten songs and actually received eleven. (One of the most well-known hidden tracks of all time is Nirvana's song "Endless, Nameless," which appears at the end of their blockbuster 1991 album *Nevermind*, but only after a whopping ten minutes of complete silence! How cool is that?)

This led me to think, wouldn't it be cool to have a hidden chapter in a book? You thought you were getting a mere thirty-three chapters, when suddenly you turned the last page of chapter one and discovered a hidden chapter you didn't even pay for.

You're welcome.

I do have another, more sober reason for adding this hidden chapter, however. Several weeks after I finished this manuscript, somebody made the following observation: "You wrote a book about . . . yourself? Isn't that, like, a vanity project?"

I didn't see that one coming. Me? Engaged in a vanity project?

But maybe my reader had a point. Standard autobiography may work if you're a movie star or former president—but a fictional narrative in which you write yourself in as the main character? That could be viewed as sufficiently self-absorbed to warrant a Carly Simon lyric: "You're so vain I bet you wrote this book all about you." And I certainly wouldn't want to be lumped in with the likes of Warren Beatty (or whomever Simon was actually singing about—the debates on that continue).

The reader who raised the concern offered an easy way out. I could simply write myself out of the book and offer the job to a fictional apologist. Sure, that would be easy. Use "find/replace" to substitute every reference to "Randal" with "Maximus" or "Apollos" or even "Billy Bob" and I could solve the perceived problem in minutes. But while this was worthy of consideration, I decided to keep myself in the book. But why, you may ask, apart from heretofore unacknowledged megalomaniacal impulses?

First, I don't want any unnecessary barriers between you and me. I want this book to provide an example of how *I* might engage in an extended grande conversation. So why at the last minute would I invite some guy I don't even know onstage and hand him my script?

Second, putting myself in the coffee shop allows me the luxury of drawing on my own personal experiences and examples. For instance, in chapter twenty-nine I discuss what I call "LAMPs" (little amazing moments of providence)—experiences people have had of God acting in their lives. In the chapter I share real-life examples that my students at the seminary where I teach have shared with me. And I'm not about to let some fictional apologist claim my real-life examples as his own.

Finally, I don't think the end product reads like a vanity project. I've tried to write an authentic conversation in which my interlocutor hits pretty hard and I don't always have satisfactory answers. My goal is not to compose an essay rubbed to a fine burnish but rather to chronicle the living, breathing reality of real, extended truth-seeking.

In other words, I tried to write a grande conversation.

What that means is that I have the occasional bad argument, lame joke, poor reaction and unwise comment. But what I hope is that in the midst of this tangled labyrinth of the good, the bad and the banal, an abiding commitment to be honest and seek truth shines through. Because at the end of the apologetics day, humbly seeking truth is the only thing worth chasing.

Are my reasons for keeping myself in the book enough to persuade you? I hope so. But even if you still find my presence at the Beatnik Bean a bit vain, I hope you can forgive my character fault (hey, nobody's perfect) and get something out of the conversation nonetheless.

One more word before we sit down, dear Reader, and it's a bit of a spoiler. I begin this book a Christian, and I end it a Christian. My grande conversation changes me, grows me and modifies what I think, but it doesn't ultimately convert me to another religious or philosophical commitment.

However, this is a real conversation—and so is my life. If you aren't a Christian, consider this the beginning of a relationship. E-mail me. Call me. Set up your sleeping bag outside my office. (Okay, maybe one of the first two options would be best.) In any case, talk to me. If you've read this far, then both of us are passionate about pursuing what is true.

And with that, I do believe it's time to order our drinks and find a few comfortable chairs at the Beatnik Bean.

2

Why a Good Argument Ain't Such a Bad Thing

* * *

Here we are. The Beatnik Bean!"

It's a cool spring morning, the streets fresh with last night's rain. We walk past the wrought-iron tables on the sidewalk—too uncomfortable for an extended conversation and, given the traffic, also too noisy—and enter the dark interior of the Beatnik Bean. The aroma of freshly ground coffee beans, sharp and savory, overpowers us. The lazy saxophone of Stan Getz on the speakers melds with the steady hum of conversation and the occasional hiss and wheeze of the espresso machine. We weave between the tables and over to the fireplace where I flop down on the couch. You, dear Reader, opt for a dramatic wing chair that looks like it was borrowed from Dracula's castle.

I grin. "Did I choose the right place or what? How many Starbucks boast an old gas fireplace that offers the flicker of flames to facilitate those 'Eureka!' moments of intellectual inspiration? Not many, I'll tell you that."

The bookshelf behind your chair is stacked with a number of

volumes in a self-regulated library. But not the standard Tom Clancy and *Chicken Soup for the Soul* stuff you might expect to find in a lesser establishment. Instead, the Beatnik Bean boasts a shelf crammed with paper and ink heavyweights like Plato's *Republic*, the *Tao Te Ching* and Descartes's *Meditations*. Above the bookshelf is a sign that reads, "Think great thoughts, read great books."

"What did I tell you, eh? This place is ideal."

As you begin to leaf through a worn copy of *Philosophy Now* that's sitting on the coffee table—or you might be doodling in it, for all I know—I get up to order us a couple of the Beatnik Bean's famous Americanos. The barista, whose name tag declares, "Hi, I'm Ashank," greets me with a friendly nod. "Hey, how you doing? What can I get you?"

"Two quad-shot Americanos," I reply. "And two of your carrot muffins."

Ashank pauses. "You know, our Americanos are pretty strong. You sure you want four shots?"

"Not want," I reply. "Need. We've got a lot of talking to do."

Ashank grins. "You bet." As he goes over to make the coffee, The Who's classic song "The Seeker" begins to play with its haunting description of a wandering soul searching for the meaning of life.

I bring the two steaming mugs and the muffins back to the coffee table. I smile with anticipation. "I can't wait to get into a great argument!"

The arch of your eyebrows suggests that you see an inconsistency between seeking truth as an apologist and relishing a good argument. "Don't worry," I add. "It's true that the word 'argument' has some negative connotations, since it tends to conjure up images of red-faced people with bulging eyes and flecks of spit flying from their mouths."

I take a sip of coffee and nearly burn my mouth. "But I'm thinking of 'argument' in terms of its etymology. The verb 'to argue' comes from a Latin root meaning 'to make clear.' I have no desire to bulge any veins or pump any adrenaline today, believe me, but I have a great interest in a first-class argument in the dogged pursuit of truth.

"Now," I say around the sides of my muffin, "dig in!"

3

The Grande Conversation Begins

* * *

You ask me what happens next, and I tell you the answer is simple. "We just have to wait for somebody with a dissenting belief system to walk into the Beatnik Bean so we can begin our grande conversation!"

Your eyebrows are arching again, but I soldier on. "I think today we should look for an atheist-skeptic type since the secular worldview constitutes the most serious challenge to Christianity in the West. While we're waiting, let me share a tip for getting the grande conversation going: Employ strategically placed conversation starters. For example . . ." I reach into my book bag and pull out a shiny silver copy of Richard Dawkins's bestseller *The God Delusion*. "No atheist can walk by without sharing a comment on Dawkins."

With that, I place the book prominently on the edge of the pitted coffee table, slightly propped up by the corner of a couple of *Mother Jones* magazines for better visibility.

"Here's another conversation starter," I say as I open my laptop. Pasted on the back of the case are two stickers, a Darwin fish and an ichthus. I tap the stickers. "Great catalysts for conversation since many people still pit Darwin against God. Whatever your views on that topic, these two stickers are bound to get people talking. That's the great thing about having a laptop. You can treat it like a portable billboard. Set up shop pretty much anywhere, pop the lid with your evocative stickers, and wait. The possibilities are endless. Just imagine the inquiries if you plastered on an 'Anarchists for Jesus' bumper sticker!"

This is going to be a long day if you keep doing that thing with your eyebrows.

At that moment the bell over the door rings and a young man walks into the darkened interior of the Beatnik Bean. He looks like a graduate student in his mid-twenties with a ponytail, wire-rimmed glasses, a backpack and a T-shirt silkscreened with a smiling Jesus giving a thumbs-up sign. Under the picture is this provocative caption: "There's a sucker born again every minute." You glance over at me and I whisper, "Talk about portable billboards! Looks like that's our guy."

As we casually sip our drinks, the thumbs-up Jesus guy buys a dark French roast and a rhubarb muffin. Then he spins around and walks over to the cream and sugar. As he passes our little enclave I hold up Dawkins's *The God Delusion* and make like I'm intently reading. Thumbs-up Jesus guy notices the glint of the silver cover, distinguishable even in dim light.

"Hey, cool," he says over his shoulder as he stirs a dollop of cream into his coffee. "You're reading Dawkins, huh? That's a pretty sweet book."

"Yeah, I guess," I reply noncommittally. "For a biologist, anyway. So what's with the thumbs-up Jesus?"

"Huh?" Our guest looks confused until I point to his shirt. He looks down and the confusion is dispelled. "Oh, I forgot I was wearing this shirt." Suddenly he looks at me suspiciously. "You're not a sucker, are you?"

"Well, I'm not sure I like your options," I reply. "Is it possible to be born again and not be a sucker?"

Thumbs-up Jesus guy smiles at us and extends a hand. "Probably not, but don't take it personally. I'm Sheridan."

I take his hand. "Sheridan? That's an interesting name."

"Yeah, it's Irish. It means 'seeker.'"

"Hm, seeker, eh?" I smile. "My name's Randal." I gesture toward you. "This is Reader."

Sheridan looks at you quizzically. "Your name's Reader? And you think my name is interesting?"

"So what is it with this sucker business?" I ask.

Sheridan laughs. "Why are you so interested? You must be a Christian, right? Did you see the film *Religulous* where Bill Maher pokes fun at religion?"

"Pokes fun at?" I reply. "I could have sworn he was mocking it."

Sheridan smirks. "Interesting, you're the first faith-head I've met that saw it. And it didn't bother you when Maher pointed out there's no evidence that Jesus even existed?"

I almost fall out of my chair. "I hope you're kidding, Sheridan. Bill Maher is a—say it with me—a comedian, an entertainer, not a historian. You don't exactly see him going head to head with leading scholars, do you? Remember the scene when Maher drops in on some humble truckers meeting at a roadside chapel so that he can mock their faith?"

"Mock?" Sheridan looks indignant. "I found him quite respectful."

"Oh, very respectful. Is it any surprise that the truckers can't challenge Maher in a conversation that he's scripted and in which they're ad-libbing? They know Freightliners, not philosophy. Who did Maher convince with that besides the already convinced?"

"Hey, they're big boys, Randal. They can take care of themselves."

"Here's a question for you, Sheridan. How many tenured professors of ancient history doubt the existence of Jesus?"

"Most, I would guess," Sheridan replies curtly. "Except at Bible schools, of course."

"Keep guessing," I say. "Here's a scene that would have been perfect for the director's cut: Bill Maher, the comedian, telling

Paul Maier, the Russell H. Seibert Professor of Ancient History at Western Michigan University, that Jesus never existed. Then we could all laugh—respectfully, of course—at Bill Maher."

"Okay, I'm getting the vibe that you don't like being called a 'sucker.' So then what should I call religious people like you? You believe in a sky God who sits on a throne above and governs the world like a petty potentate. You can believe that if you want to, but if it doesn't make you a sucker, then what does it make you? Why not believe in Zeus or Thor instead? There are countless gods of the ancient world. The Christian God just happens to have a following. No doubt that's just good luck."

"Oh yeah, no doubt," I reply, albeit with more sarcasm than I should probably be using.

"Your Yahweh trinity God may have survived thus far, Randal, but rewind the tape of history and run it again and Zeus or Thor might have two billion followers today while your God would be an obscure footnote in religious history textbooks."

"That's an interesting assertion, Sheridan."

"Here's something even more interesting. Imagine for a minute that you're walking down the street and a man approaches you proclaiming the religion of the 'sacred four-leaf clover.' Since you're obviously a fellow who enjoys engaging others in religious blather, you ask him to describe his god for you. So this dude starts babbling self-importantly about how he worships a divine quaternity, a god made up of four distinct and equally divine beings. He then goes on to explain with deadly seriousness that his sacred four-leaf clover is composed of an invisible leaping leprechaun, a centaur, a mermaid and a spotted unicorn named Bree Har. To top it off, he piously intones, 'Four in one and one in four, sacred four-leaf clover be praised, amen.'

"Look, dude," Sheridan says with a snicker. "You wouldn't take this guy seriously for one second. Heck, you'd be doing well not to burst out laughing after his earnest little theology lesson. But is

Christianity really any less fantastic than this? You believe there's one God who is three distinct persons and each of those persons has a title and description no less bizarre than those of the sacred four-leaf clover. Divine trinity? Divine clover? The only difference is that your deity is more familiar to you. So what? A mom who's drunk before noon may be familiar to the child of an alcoholic. That doesn't make her a normal parent."

I look over at you. "Yikes," I say with a disarming grin. "That's a pretty stark comparison."

"Hey, I'm just getting started," Sheridan continues. "Your definition of God is only the beginning of your bizarre claims. From the talking snake in the garden to the flying city in Revelation, the Bible is a collection of children's stories that make Aesop's fables look like deathly serious literature by comparison."

"Sheridan, I know we just met, but please, don't hold back on account of my feelings," I say. "Tell us what you really think."

Sheridan shrugs. "I guess I just want religious people to be a bit more rational about their beliefs every once in a while. That's all I'm asking."

There's an uncomfortable silence for a moment. Just as you begin to think this might be the end of the conversation, I speak up. "Sheridan, why don't you join us? We're up for a talk on the meaning of life. Another voice in the conversation would be a nice addition."

Sheridan shrugs. "Sure, I guess. I don't have any big plans."

As he pulls up a chair he winks and says, "I might as well see if I can sort you two out."

4

"Reasonable" Scientists, "Deluded" Believers and the Quest for Objectivity

✷ ✷ ✷

After settling down, Sheridan leans toward me and says seriously, "You know why you can't get the fact that your beliefs are so weird? Because you're not objective about them."

"Wait a minute, Sheridan," I say. "You met me about five minutes ago and you already know that I'm not being objective in my beliefs? How does that work?"

"Hey, don't look so shocked. You make judgments like that about other people all the time."

"I do?" I ask. "So you know how I think? Where do you keep your crystal ball?"

"No, dude, I don't believe in magic like you do. I'm just making an educated guess. Look, instead of getting indignant, just tell me if I'm wrong. Here's the picture. You're walking down the street trying to find your way to a new restaurant. Just as you realize you're lost, you see this guy walking toward you. He's got a long frazzled beard and wild eyes and he's like mumbling stuff to himself. When he notices your apparent confusion, he walks up and offers to give you directions. Would you accept the offer?" Sheridan takes a long drink of his French roast as he waits for me to respond.

"Probably not," I reply.

Sheridan nods with satisfaction. "That's what I'm talking about."

"Unless," I add, "he could demonstrate that he's mentally balanced. For instance, I might believe him if I learned that he was an actor preparing for an evening performance of *Macbeth*. If he could offer a plausible explanation for his unusual behavior and if the directions he offered made sense, then I probably would listen to him."

Sheridan rolls his eyes. "Uh oh—by that answer I can tell you're either a lawyer or a philosopher."

"Theologian, actually," I reply. "I teach at a seminary."

"Why am I not surprised? Okay, listen. Forget your 'actor' idea. All you know is that some crazy-looking guy offers to give you directions. That's it. Do you accept the offer or not? And remember, your judgment is based on less than five minutes of contact."

I feign a look of dismay. "So you think Christians are the equivalent of mentally unstable street people? I'm deeply hurt."

Sheridan laughs. "Yeah, I can see the tears welling up in your eyes." He looks over at you. "And it looks like Reader here is speechless. My point is simply that five minutes or less can tell you a lot about how stable a person is."

"And you just know that we're a bunch of unstable suckers?"

Sheridan nods. "Precisely. If you weren't, this conversation would have ended with my sacred four-leaf clover illustration, because you would have immediately recognized the absurdity of your beliefs. Look, if I told you that gal—" he gestures toward a young woman texting on her phone at a nearby table—"believes the Holocaust never happened, you'd draw some pretty harsh conclusions about her character right away, without ever talking with her or considering the evidence she might offer for her skepticism.

So don't be so surprised when I draw some conclusions about you after I hear that you believe in an invisible sky God. Heck, I'd say I've been quite polite so far."

"Your self-restraint is noted," I reply dryly.

Sheridan continues. "There are millions of gods worshiped out there and tens of thousands of religions, and each one claims to offer the inside track to one or more of those gods. Now think about that, man. Doesn't that bother you? Doesn't it bother you how completely arbitrary that is? If you want to see what I'm seeing, look at your beliefs in the mirror. And if you see a crazy guy with a frazzled beard staring back at you, then you'll know what I'm seeing. You have to start thinking about your beliefs like an outsider does."

"Yeah, well, you should see how you look from my perspective," I retort.

Sheridan continues without acknowledging the point. "If you want to see how crazy your beliefs really are, objectivity is the key, my friend." With that pronouncement he begins smearing butter on his precisely halved muffin.

I sit back in my chair, incredulous. "Are you saying I need to approach all my beliefs like that? As an outsider?"

"No, not all of them," Sheridan says between chews. "Some beliefs are reasonable because they're open to evidence and confirmation. But others are not. Those are the ones you need to worry about. The more outlandish the belief, the more you should reflect objectively on it. And before you get all defensive, Randal, just stop and think about how sensible that is."

Sheridan gestures again to the young woman at the nearby table, who is still texting on her phone. "Let's say I told you that she's a follower of Zeus, king of the Olympian gods. She believes the details of Greek mythology as if they were true and she faithfully participates in the sacrifice of bulls to appease Zeus so she won't get hit by a lightning bolt. If you knew that, would you hire her to do your taxes or to housesit when you go on vacation?"

"Sacrificing bulls, eh?" I reply. "Well, before inviting her to housesit I'd want to make sure my dogs would be safe."

"Dude, I'm serious. The truth is that you wouldn't have anything to do with her because you know, along with all other enlightened residents of the twenty-first century, that Zeus is a mythological deity. Right, Reader?" Sheridan casts you a piercing sidelong glance and then continues.

"What lets Christians off the rationality hook? That gal may be worshiping some obsolete deity from Mount Olympus, and you happen to be worshipping Yahweh, a deity from a different ancient religion. But really, what's the difference?"

"What do you say it is?" I reply.

"I already told you. While Zeus's religion died out, your God still has a couple billion followers due to a bit of historical luck and happenstance."

I lean forward. "Two billion, eh? That's quite a big difference though, isn't it?"

"If what two billion people believe could make your God exist it would be a huge difference, but unfortunately for you truth isn't decided by committee. You're hiding in a crowd of weirdoes pretending to be normal. The only thing that makes you think you're more rational than the lone worshiper of Zeus is that you're one of two billion. Your Christian books, music and churches all reinforce your beliefs. My religious stepfather even buys 'Testamints' for fresh and holy breath. Think about it: even your breath mints reinforce your crazy beliefs."

Sheridan takes another bite of muffin. "You're living inside a bubble—you end up thinking your beliefs make sense only because everyone you interact with also believes them. But if you bothered to poke your head out of your little bubble, you'd see how ridiculous you look. Believe me, I know what I'm talking about firsthand."

Sheridan begins to count off his fingers. "Christian camp and vacation Bible school in the summer, Christmas pageant in the winter, Easter pageant in the spring, church services, Bible studies and youth group every week. It was all so reasonable. It was only when I started asking questions that nobody wanted to answer that I began to see how weird the whole thing really is."

Sheridan pauses, pats me on the shoulder and then continues with mock seriousness, "Sorry to tell you, Randal, but you are seriously deluded."

In the background the jazz guitar of Kenny Burrell and the hiss of the espresso machine fill in the silence as I take a moment to mull Sheridan's argument and the snippets of personal biography that have come with it. Since it seems like he's said his piece for the moment, I begin to talk.

"Sheridan, you're certainly right that beliefs that seem outrageous are reinforced by a shared plausibility framework. If nobody else shares your religious beliefs, it's very difficult to sustain them. You clearly find my beliefs weird, but then, as I pointed out a minute ago, I find many of your beliefs to be weird. Your beliefs may make sense within your plausibility framework—which is also reinforced by your own bubble effect, by the way—but not within mine. So there's no neutral way to judge whose beliefs are 'weird.' That judgment is always made relative to a set of beliefs that the person making the judgment accepts. Both of us do that."

Sheridan looks dismissive. "That sounds quite postmodern to me," he says. "It's also way too pessimistic. The fact is that we have a great way to sort out which beliefs are worth holding—and which are weird."

I hold out my hand invitingly. "Please, enlighten me."

"Science," Sheridan replies matter-of-factly. "Scientists everywhere agree on the basic facts. Haven't you noticed that we don't have one kind of science in the United States and another in Indonesia? One science doesn't apply in Asia and another in Europe.

There isn't one science for men and another for women, or one for the rich and another for the poor. It's all about comparing theory to fact, period."

As Sheridan speaks I paste an incredulous look on my face, hoping to communicate just how naïve and precritical I find his understanding of scientific enquiry. But he soldiers on, undeterred. "Unlike scientific beliefs, however, religious beliefs are geographically distributed. If you're born in Indonesia, you'll probably be a Muslim, while if you're born in America you'll probably be raised a Christian."

"Especially if you're born in Kentucky or Oklahoma," I add.

Sheridan nods. "Exactly! And if you're born in India? Hindu. And so on. That geographic distribution makes it pretty clear that religion isn't objective. It's all about indoctrination, about being told what to believe until you believe it. In that way it's like other aspects of culture like music, dress, food and art. You like and believe what you're raised with. The only way to get beyond your indoctrination is by subjecting your beliefs to the critical eye of an outsider."

When Sheridan pauses to breathe I ask, "And if I do that, what will happen?"

"Simple. You'll see that belief in Jesus is as arbitrary and irrational as belief in Zeus."

5

What Must You Do to
See a Buffalo or Cast a Vote?

* * *

Sheridan grins and takes swig of coffee, then reaches into his backpack and pulls out a book called *The Christian Delusion*. "I've actually got some stuff on this right here." He flips about a third of the way into the book. "Here's how John Loftus, a well-known atheist who formulated the outsider test for faith, puts it."

With that Sheridan looks down to read. "His first point is that 'rational people in distinct geographical locations around the globe overwhelmingly adopt and defend a wide diversity of religious faiths due to their upbringing and cultural heritage.' Like I said, undoubtedly true, right? Just look on a map that shows religious affiliation and you'll see what I mean."

Before I can get a word in, he continues reading. "'Consequently, it seems very likely that adopting one's religious faith is not merely a matter of independent rational judgment but is causally dependent on cultural conditions to an overwhelming degree.'"

Sheridan is getting excited now, perching on the edge of his chair and reading faster and faster. "'Hence the odds are highly

likely," here he punches the air for emphasis, "that any given ad-
opted religious faith is false."[2]

He smiles. "Seems to me you ought to take that challenge. Try
to subject your beliefs to that kind of critical analysis. When you
do, you'll come to see the light. I've got at least that much faith in
your rational ability."

Sheridan looks over at you. "You too, Reader. You're not off the
hook just because you're so quiet. I assume that if you're with this
guy then you've got some weird religious beliefs as well. That is,
unless you're another one of Randal's evangelism projects."

"There does seem to be some evangelism happening today," I
say, "but let's get back to what you just read. I take it that the outsider test is supposed to challenge people to think critically about
their beliefs?"

"That's the whole point!"

"Well, given that the goal of your challenge is consistent rational belief—as an objective outsider would see it—I assume you
won't mind if I apply some critical thinking to the test as you've
posed it?"

"Sure, just so long as you're not trying to rationalize your beliefs. Remember, you're the one who needs to take the test."

"Maybe so, maybe not," I reply. "That's yet to be decided, I
think. See, I find myself stumbling at the second premise. What
makes the level of a religion's causal dependence on culture
'overwhelming'? How would one judge that? You need to defend
that premise. You can't just assume it, because I find no reason
to accept it. So tell me, why do you think cultural influence is
'overwhelming'?"

"That's special pleading, Randal."

"Not at all!" I exclaim. "All our knowledge and beliefs are
shaped by our cultural environment. Take vision, for example."
With that I stand up and walk over to a young man sitting on a
couch studying intently for final exams. On the table is a stack of

books on psychology, including Lionel Nicholas's *Introduction to Psychology*. "Could I borrow this for a moment?" I ask.

The young man looks up. "Sure," he replies wearily. "And don't feel obliged to bring it back anytime soon, either." He turns back to his work with a wry smile.

I take the book, set it open on the coffee table and flip through it until I find the correct page. "Nicholas is helpful on this," I say to Sheridan, "because he recounts the findings of an anthropologist named Turnbull that illustrate the extent to which perception is shaped by culture and environment. Let's see . . . here it is. 'Turnbull stated that when he was accompanied by a pygmy guide (who had spent his entire life in the dense jungle . . . never entering the plains in any manner) onto the open plains, they observed a buffalo (which the pygmy had only ever seen at a maximum distance of 30 meters in the jungle). When the pygmy was shown the buffalo at a distance he asked what kind of insect it was. When told that it was not an insect but rather a buffalo, he stated that it could not be a buffalo as it was too small.'"[3]

I close the book and look at Sheridan. "This striking event taught Turnbull something of the extent to which perception is shaped by culture and context. A person raised in a dense jungle will perceive particular sensory stimuli as a nearby insect while somebody raised on the plain will interpret the same stimuli as a distant buffalo."

Sheridan looks dumbfounded. "Wait a minute, Randal. Are you saying that one man's insect is another man's buffalo?"

"Not quite. In this case one description is clearly correct and the other is false—it really was a buffalo. But this story shows that our perceptual judgments are not free of context. All of our experience of the world is deeply formed by culture and experience."

Sheridan shrugs. "I still don't see the relevance of this example for religion."

"The point is that sensory perceptions are distributed over geographic regions in much the same way religious perceptions are. As I said, people living in the jungle interpret a particular sense experience as seeing an insect, whereas people on the plains interpret that same sense experience as seeing a buffalo. What you perceive depends on the culture and environment in which you were raised. Who knows to what extent living in North America today might have shaped our perception of things? But even though we know that perception is shaped by our culture and experience, we don't thereby cast doubt on all our perception. After all, the guy that reported he saw a buffalo was correct. Instead we should adopt an 'innocent until proven guilty' attitude, recognizing that perception is generally trustworthy even if it is not infallible. Why not think about religious beliefs in similar terms? Couldn't they also be generally trustworthy even though they too are shaped by culture and environment? I mean, we're not obliged to adopt some kind of 'outsider test' before we can accept our sense perceptions, are we? So why must we with our religious perceptions?"

Sheridan lets a disdainful puff of air escape his lips. "Look, scientists agree about what they perceive. Religions don't."

Even though I feel a tinge of frustration, I continue to smile. "Sheridan, that's not as true as you seem to think. Thomas Kuhn pointed out half a century ago in *The Structure of Scientific Revolutions* that the scientist's perception of data is conditioned by the paradigm or model by which she interprets the data. In one example, Kuhn notes that a massive nova that exploded in the Middle Ages was recorded by Chinese astronomers but not European ones. Why do you think that was?"

Sheridan shrugs. "I guess they couldn't see it from Europe."

"Actually, they could. They didn't record it because of their assumptions based on Greek cosmology that the heavens are static and don't change. Once they assumed that the cosmos was static, they screened out any evidence to the contrary, including the flash of a nova."

Sheridan's brow furrows skeptically. "Are you saying that they didn't see anything? Medieval Europeans were blind to novas? So then if they didn't believe in the moon then they wouldn't see that either?"

"I'm not saying that. I don't doubt that they saw something. But their assumptions about what they should see led them to dismiss the very same phenomenon that was carefully recorded by the Chinese. We shouldn't underestimate the extent to which expectation affects perception. Sometimes we really do filter out data— and sometimes we do the opposite and our minds fill in the blanks and we end up seeing something that isn't there."

"How so?"

"Ever watch a horror flick late at night?"

"Oh yeah, I love horror films. *The Shining* is one of my favorites."

"Then you probably know that after watching a film like that you're hypersensitive to stimuli, and as a result you can start 'seeing' and 'hearing' all sorts of things. The slightest movement in the corner of your eye becomes a ghostly apparition, and a barely noticeable creak on the stairs suddenly becomes the stealthy approach of a knife-wielding maniac.

"And here's an everyday example without the movie mumbo-jumbo," I continue. "We have a small white dog. I can't count the number of times I've seen the dog sitting on the carpet out of the corner of my eye, but when I turn I realize I was just seeing a white cushion. Since I expect to see a white dog my brain imposes that pattern on all sorts of fuzzy white lumps.

"So the way we perceive the world, just like religion, reflects a geographical pattern," I say. "But we don't use that fact as a reason to constantly mistrust our senses. If I think I see a red apple on the counter, then all things being equal I'm surely right to believe that I'm seeing that apple. If geographical distribution and cultural formation aren't grounds to automatically doubt my senses, why are they grounds to doubt religious belief?"

I'm ready for Sheridan to respond, but when he doesn't say anything for a few moments I decide to try something a bit more aggressive. "I do think your demand for an outsider test goes way beyond what the data warrants—but in another sense you aren't even going far enough."

That gets Sheridan's attention. "What do you mean by that?"

"I mean that if you're going to apply a skeptical outsider test to a person's religion, you should apply it to their other beliefs, too. Take politics: what system do you accept?"

"Representational democracy. Not that we have it here in the West. We're slaves to the corporatocracy."

"Uh, okay . . . so representational democracy it is. But don't you believe in representational democracy because you're an American? If you were born into Afghanistan or North Korea or Saudi Arabia, do you think you'd have been an advocate of representative democracy? The fact is that political theories are also largely distributed over geographic areas. So if I accept your outsider test in religion, then it applies here as well, and you need to test your political convictions with the outsider test as surely as does the Afghani, North Korean or Saudi Arabian."

Sheridan thinks for a moment. "I have no problem with that, I guess."

"Really? But applying it consistently to all our beliefs is impossible."

"Impossible? Why?"

"Just think about the implications for politics. Even if you could defend representational democracy over and against other systems, you wouldn't be done. In fact, you'd just be getting started! Then you'd have to defend your chosen political party. After all, party affiliation is also deeply influenced by geography. Consider Uriah, born and raised in Provo, Utah. He's from good Mormon stock, and just like his state, Uriah is staunchly conservative Republican."

Sheridan makes a crass gagging sound, signaling his distaste for Mormons, Republicans or both.

I continue. "But then there's Sig, born and raised in Portland, Oregon. Sig uses only kosher sea salt on his vegetarian tofu frittatas and is a secular and politically liberal Democrat, just like his state."

"Woo-hoo!" Sheridan cheers. "That's more like it," he says.

"Okay," I say with a grin, "your sympathies are clear. But this all means that before an election, Uriah and Sig have to defend not only their commitment to representational democracy but also to their political party. What would that even look like? Maybe Uriah and Sig should try something like that reality television show *Wife Swap*, where each wife goes to live in the other's constituency for a month. Does that make sense? Are we really obliged to test our political commitments like this before we can cast a vote?"

"Obviously that's extreme," Sheridan replies. "However, the general idea is a good one. We should test our political allegiances. I'm pretty confident that a reasonable person would come out favoring representational democracy. And a reasonable person who submitted their religion to the outsider test would become an atheist."

"That sounds reasonable, Sheridan—reasonable just like the assumption that anybody who truly submitted their favorite type of music to the outsider test would eventually be converted to polka, because obviously music just doesn't get better than America's polka king Frankie Yankovic."

6

God, Matter and Other Astonishing Hypotheses

* * *

Jarred back to the point of our conversation by the imagined sounds of a polka band, Sheridan returns to the idea of culture and geography.

"Sorry, Randal," he says, "but your focus on the geographical distribution of perceptual and political beliefs breaks down at a crucial point."

"Which is?"

"Representational democracy makes good sense to people not already indoctrinated with some other ideology. But your religious beliefs don't. They're bizarre. Why can't you see that you're trying to bring worship of a petty tribal god from the ancient world into the modern age, and it just doesn't fit?"

Sheridan scans the coffee shop, mentally searching for an analogy. "It's like you're trying to sell a dusty old phonograph at a tech conference. You shouldn't be surprised when people opt to stick with their laptops and smartphones."

I can't help but laugh at the image of a person comparison shopping in Sheridan's simile. "Phonograph? Now that's pretty funny."

"You like that, huh?" he says with a grin. "Well, don't laugh too much, dude, because you're the punch line."

"Hey, hold up. You keep ignoring the fact that your beliefs look weird to me. Why doesn't that count?"

"Oh, come on!" Sheridan grabs my shoulder. "I believe in science. Don't tell me you're going to call science weird. You benefit from it every day, all the time, as you enjoy the benefits of technology." Sheridan points toward the coffee bar. "You think you could have your beloved espresso shots without science? If you got rid of science altogether you'd still be sitting in a cave drinking swamp water!"

"Swamp water? What's the link there, exactly?"

"Forget about trying to dis science, bro. Just look at your beliefs for a minute. You believe in some spooky ghost who's just, like, out there and who knows everything and controls everything. You honestly can't see how that looks nutso to other people?"

"Sheridan, you're not showing a whole lot of charity in your characterization of my beliefs. How about this for an incredible belief: a universe that sprung into existence out of nothing about fourteen billion years ago. You don't think that's unbelievable?"

Sheridan stares at me. "So now you're rejecting the big bang? That's one of the most well-attested theories in science!"

"No, you're missing the point. I accept the big bang, but that doesn't change the fact that it's an incredible claim."

"Look, I suggest you read Vic Stenger's book *God: The Astonishing Hypothesis*. He'll give you a sense of just how crazy you look trying to peddle your phonograph at a tech convention."

"Actually, I've read that book. And I'm glad you mentioned it because it helps me make my point. Stenger's claim that God is an 'astonishing' hypothesis is doubly flawed. Stenger gets the nature of Christian belief about God all wrong. For Christians, God isn't a hypothesis; he's a living, experienced reality. And Stenger's labeling of belief in God as 'astonishing' is just self-serving. As I've been saying, the fact is that everybody finds certain beliefs held by others to be 'astonishing.' So the mere fact that you find a certain belief I hold to be astonishing, or 'nutso,' isn't a real argument against the belief. It's just a comment on your personal psychology."

Sheridan yawns and rolls his eyes. "There's your postmodernism again," he says.

"Careful, Sheridan." I say with a touch of frustration. "Slapping a broad label like postmodernism across the particular views of others can be an excuse for not thinking hard."

"That's pretty ironic commentary coming from a fundamentalist," Sheridan snaps back.

As I raise my eyebrows in surprise, he begins to laugh. "Just kidding, dude! I won't call you a pomo anymore."

"Or a fundamentalist?" I add hopefully.

"Hey, no promises on that one," he replies, smirking.

"Well, okay," I say and sigh. "I guess that's the most I can hope for given that you're a pagan."

Sheridan looks impressed. "I must say it's my pleasure to trade insults with you. Too many of the fundies I meet are super uptight."

"Anyway," I say, "forget about Vic Stenger's *God: The Astonishing Hypothesis*. Consider instead a book by Sic Venger called *Matter: The Astonishing Hypothesis*."

"Sic Venger?" Sheridan snorts. "This is going to be good, I can tell."

"Venger," I continue, "is a proponent of the philosophical theory of idealism."

"Idealism?" Sheridan squints like he's trying to jog his memory. "How about a definition? It's been a couple years since I took an Intro Phil class."

"Sure," I reply. "Idealism is the view that matter does not exist. All that exists are minds and their 'ideas.'"

"And what's an 'idea'?"

"An idea is any object of conscious experience: the smell of a rose, the taste of coffee or the color of a barn. Our entire experience of the world is a bewilderingly complex flow of these ideas. And the idealist is saying that's all we need. We don't need to posit a physical rose, coffee or barn 'out there' to explain our experience. All that exists are our minds and these ideas they experience."

Sheridan looks at me dismissively. "So that's idealism? Kind of like being caught in the matrix, huh? No wonder I didn't keep studying philosophy."

"You think idealism is weird," I say, "and that's exactly my point. Idealism can explain everything we experience without ever having to posit the existence of matter. So you reject it because it strikes you as weird, not because you have an argument against it."

"What? Are you freaking kidding me?" Sheridan laughs so hard that people from nearby tables look over. Then he raps his knuckles on the table with visible disdain. "Here's an argument against it. What do you think I'm knocking on, dude? An idea in my head?"

I hold up a hand. "Hey, take a breath. You don't seriously think that idealists are unaware of the sensations of feeling and hearing wood being rapped on, do you? That coffee table you knocked on is a great way to illustrate the idealist thesis. Look at the table. What do you see?"

Sheridan answers tersely. "A deeply worn wood grain and countless coffee stains."

"What do you feel?"

Sheridan looks noticeably impatient. "A hard table, man. Heck, what do you feel?"

Since I can tell I'm losing my audience, I skip to the bottom line. "The idealist argues that when you add it all up, our experience of the table simply amounts to a bundle of sensations like the color, texture and smell of the wood."

"I recommend you don't add taste to your list," Sheridan says, snickering. "It looks like it's been a while since this baby was wiped down."

"Don't worry—no point is so important that I'll start licking the furniture!"

I hold up my half-drunk Americano. "The experience of drinking coffee is a bundle of smells, textures, colors, tastes and other sensations." I nod toward the window with the afternoon sun streaming in. "There you have the warmth and glare of the sun. Just more sensations." I point toward the table. "And the taste and texture of your precious rhubarb muffin—or at least what remains of it. And on and on. The idealist argues that we don't ever experience matter itself. Matter is just a mysterious extended substance that we posit as supposedly lying behind the sensations. But all we actually experience are the sensations, so sensations are really all we need to explain our experience."

Sheridan looks mystified. "I just don't get it. So what is it that we are supposed to be experiencing? What are these sensations of?"

"Idealists answer that question in different ways. The most famous idealist was the eighteenth-century philosopher George Berkeley. He argued that God immediately acts on human minds to create sensations. That provided a way for Berkeley to stress the world's radical dependence on God. The taste of the rhubarb muffin and glare of the sun and smell of the espresso all come from direct divine action on the mind. There is no muffin or sun or espresso beyond the muffin, sun and espresso sensations that God places in our minds."

Sheridan is still chewing on this. "So there is no world? Just sensations?"

"Not quite. Rather, the world *is* minds and their sensations. There simply is no need to posit the additional supposition of matter or extended substance."

Sheridan shakes his head. "That's the wackiest thing I've heard this semester. And I took a feminist course on 'Deconstructing the Barbie Doll.'"

I can't help but smile. "Now that sounds profound. Berkeley's idealism was used as an argument for God's existence, but other idealists have been atheists. In fact, our friend Sic Venger is an atheistic idealist and he thinks he has great reasons to be one."

"Okay, I'll play along. What are his reasons?"

"Well, like many atheists, Venger rejected the existence of God based on the premise that atheism is a simpler explanation. It gives us the same world that we experience but with fewer explanatory layers. Then he realized that if simplicity was a sweeping goal that could be used to exclude God, it can and should also be used to eliminate the world of matter. Venger realized he could do scientific research all day long and enjoy a snifter of port and a cigar in the evening without ever having to invoke the objective existence of matter as a hypothesis to explain his experiences. Thus, he concluded that the 'matter hypothesis' is every bit as astonishing and unnecessary as the 'God hypothesis.' He agrees with Stenger—he just doesn't believe Stenger goes far enough."

I've talked so long that Sheridan expects me to keep right on talking. So I do.

"The alternative to Venger's idealism, the view that you and I hold—that there is a world of matter corresponding to our sensations—is called realism. Realism says that there is a world of extended substance. For most people, realism is common sense, an undeniable dimension of our ongoing experience of the world." Sheridan nods. "So do you think that Venger would win over many realists to his idealist camp simply by calling their position astonishing?"

"No, of course not."

"I agree. I'm sure they would reply that it's not matter that's astonishing but rather Venger's idealist denial of it. In fact, they'd say that matter is not a hypothesis at all. It's a natural belief that arises from our experience."

"Come on, Randal. I've been letting you throw a lot of stuff at me, but are you seriously going to compare God to matter?"

"In the relevant senses the analogy is legitimate. Our sensory experience leads us very naturally to believe in the external world. So it is for the Christian's experience of God. To believe in God is not an arbitrary, top-down explanation we force onto life. Rather, like our experience of matter, it's a natural, ground-level description of our experience of the world."

"You're not claiming to 'sense' God like you sense a cup of coffee, are you?" Sheridan smirks. "God doesn't burn your tongue if you sip him too quickly, does he?"

"He might," I shoot back, "but you're missing the most important point. As the idealist points out, matter also goes beyond the evidence since we can explain everything by appealing to minds and their ideas or sensations. So if you're a realist about the material world—if you believe there really are material objects and not just sensations—then you're in the same basic boat as the theist. While the realist finds the idealist's views astonishing, the idealist finds the realist's views astonishing. George Berkeley even argued that idealism is common sense! That means that what appears sensible to you as an atheist may be astonishing to me as a Christian and vice versa."

"I'm sorry to hear that you find science astonishing, dude. You should get out more."

"I'm less astonished by science than your atheism. My so-called postmodern claim is that judgments of astonishment are always made relative to a set of beliefs: the idealist's or the realist's or the atheist's or the Christian's or whoever's. So if you want to engage Christians more meaningfully, you should do so by attacking the core assumptions of the Christian rather than simply guffawing at how astonishing you find the so-called God hypothesis."

Sheridan looks puzzled. "Guffawing? And what is a 'guffaw,' exactly?"

"A hearty laugh," I reply shortly.

"So why not just say 'hearty laugh,' professor?"

"'Guffaw' has a nice ring to it, I guess. Look, let's keep focused. I take it that for you it is proper that people come naturally and without argument to believe there is an external world of matter."

"Sure."

"To put it another way, belief in the external world of matter can be believed rationally without evidence or reasoning. My challenge to you is to explain why belief in the external world is properly basic but belief in God cannot be."

"How do you define 'properly basic'?"

"A properly basic belief is one that you can rationally accept without appeal to evidence from other beliefs, and if it is true then you can know it, so long as you are not aware of any strong defeaters for the belief."

"And what's a defeater?"

"A defeater is evidence that appears either to 'defeat' the claim in question, either by directly contradicting it or by undermining your reasons for thinking it is true. So I don't think of Christian belief as a hypothesis that you arrive at through evidence and reasoning. Rather, it's a set of beliefs that you start out with which you may have to revise or rethink based on whatever defeaters you may encounter."

"Okay, got it. Keep going."

"Now keep in mind that I have not declared by fiat the basic rationality of religious belief. Rather, I have offered an argument comparing an atheist's analysis to an idealist's. Insofar as the latter is unconvincing, so is the former."

"I just don't accept your analogy, Randy. I don't think you can explain the world the way the idealist does. But when it comes to your metaphysics, atheism is simpler than theism. We can explain everything in the world without positing the existence of a magic sky God."

"And I don't accept that. But let's think some more about this idea of 'simpler' explanations always being preferable. *Matter: The*

Astonishing Hypothesis is just the beginning. There are all sorts of other even simpler and more astonishing hypotheses. Consider the common sense of a solipsist."

"A what?"

"Solipsists do not believe that any minds other than their own exist."

"Wait, what?" Sheridan sits up. "Seriously?"

"Yup, a solipsist believes that everything he experiences is a product of his mind. There are no other minds. To the solipsist, you and I are just aspects of his consciousness. With that in mind, a solipsist could write a book called *Other Minds: The Astonishing Hypothesis* in which he throws into doubt the very notion of minds other than his own as an unbelievable claim."

"But if he's the only person who exists, then who's he writing the book for?"

"Good point," I admit. "I guess the answer would have to be, for himself. But here's the main thing. You say atheism is a simpler hypothesis for explaining everything we experience than theism. I say that if you accept that logic then you should also become an idealist. But if you're going to go that far, why not ride all the way to Simple Town and become a solipsist?"

Sheridan rubs his forehead. "Dude, you're giving me a headache."

7

Faith

It's in the Air

Sheridan, it seems like you're trying to hold me to a standard that you don't apply to yourself," I say.

"That's a total crock," Sheridan retorts. "The double standard is all yours, buddy. I think we all need to approach our beliefs with reason. And that's all I've been asking. But you keep trying to carve out a little enclave of irrational faith for your ancient sky God."

"But Sheridan, doctrines like idealism and solipsism have been defended by highly articulate and intelligent people. And they can accommodate all the evidence we have before us. So we all take a step beyond the evidence. We can't help it. It's the human condition."

Sheridan shakes his head vigorously. "I only believe what I believe based on evidence, not faith."

"Whoa, Sheridan, really? You're claiming that you only believe things if there is evidence for them?"

Sheridan nods resolutely. "Right on, bro. I can see that's a shocking revelation for you, but that's how rational, scientific people operate. If there's evidence for something, we believe it—otherwise we don't. Religious people who teach their kids to believe without evidence are engaging in cognitive child abuse."

I look quizzical. "Can you unpack that for me? I'm apparently one of those religious people, and this is news to me."

"It's wrong to teach your kids your dogmas and faith without giving them an opportunity to think critically for themselves."

"I think I know what you're saying," I reply. "In fact, I happen to have a good example of that kind of argument." I reach into my book bag and pull out a copy of Richard Dawkins's *A Devil's Chaplain*, a collection of Dawkins's essays on religion. I hold up the book. "Have you read this?"

Sheridan looks it over with interest. "Nope."

"Well, there's an essay in here called 'Viruses of the Mind' in which Dawkins describes how his daughter was almost subjected to the tyranny of religious dogma." I look down at the book and begin to quote: "'I have just discovered that without her father's consent this sweet, trusting, gullible six-year-old is being sent, for weekly instruction, to a Roman Catholic nun. What chance has she?'"[4]

"Darn right," Sheridan nods. "Good thing he nipped that in the bud."

I close the book and put it on the table. "Sheridan, I certainly agree that there is such a thing as cognitive child abuse. For instance, teaching racial hatred to a child is unconscionable."

"How about teaching kids that they'll burn forever if they believe the wrong things?"

I nod. "Certainly that could be child abuse."

"Could be? But not necessarily?" Sheridan looks appalled.

"It depends, among other things, on whether the doctrine is true and on how it is taught."

"Oh, yeah, of course. And whether it's right to teach your kids that Jews are vermin depends on whether Jews are vermin, right? You apologists can defend any belief if you want to."

I'm itching to refute his uncalled-for "Nazi attack," but I decide instead to draw the conversation back to what I take to be the main point. "Look," I say, "I have a modest focus at the moment. I'm simply aiming to show that it's not categorically abusive to teach a child a set of religious doctrines, even if in some cases it is. Unlike Dawkins, I don't think it's abusive for a Christian parent to teach his child the Apostles' Creed or various Bible stories."

"Nope, Dawkins is right. It is abuse because you're presenting those beliefs without evidence—that's exactly what I'm challenging. It's all about the evidence. That's why it's wrong to teach kids your set of faith beliefs. You're teaching them to accept claims without evidence, and that undermines critical thinking—"

"—and can lead eight hundred people to drink cyanide-laced Kool-Aid in the Guyanan jungle," I interject.

(Just in case you're not familiar with the example, Reader, Jim Jones was a cult leader in the seventies. Back in 1978 he brought his whole flock from the States to the Guyanan jungle. When the U.S. authorities began to close in on him, he directed his entire church to commit mass suicide.)

Sheridan nods in acknowledgment. "Hey, thanks for the example. I'll be sure to use it well. So the lesson is, what begins in Sunday school ends in mass suicide."

"I agree that there are cases where people hold irrational religious beliefs that can lead them to unconscionable actions. But I want to challenge your claim that you always believe based on evidence."

"I'd like to see that," Sheridan says with a smirk. "Dig your faith hole deeper, Randal. When you finally need a reasonable, scientific hand to build you a ladder out, I'll be here, buddy."

"Okay, so you think that we should always believe in accord with evidence and reason and not believe otherwise. Correct?"

"Of course!"

"That claim has been made before. Back in 1879, mathematician W. K. Clifford published a famous essay called 'The Ethics of Belief' in which he argued that 'it is wrong everywhere, always, and for everyone to believe anything upon insufficient evidence.' Would you agree with that statement?"

Sheridan gives two thumbs up. "That Clifford sounds like a smart dude to me. Always believe the mathematician, I say." He looks at me suspiciously. "So are you suggesting that we shouldn't believe things based on evidence?"

"Before you get too committed to Clifford's maxim," I say, "you should know that it has some serious problems. Probably the most serious of all is that Clifford offers no evidence for it: he just assumes that it's true. But if we accept Clifford's maxim, then we need evidence for it since according to the maxim, we need evidence for all claims."

Sheridan looks skeptical. "That sounds like a cheap philosopher's trick."

"Expecting an assertion to follow its own rules isn't a trick. I'm pointing out that Clifford's principle is self-defeating. According to it you have to have sufficient evidence to believe anything, and that would include Clifford's principle itself. Thus, unless there is sufficient evidence supporting Clifford's principle, we must reject it. In other words, Clifford's principle shoots itself in the foot."

"That is a philosopher's trick. Why don't you come out and say it? You think we don't need evidence to believe things, right?"

"We need evidence to believe some things, but not all things. Clifford's principle is impossible to satisfy. If we require evidence for everything then we face an infinite regress since every evidence provided for a belief would itself require supporting evidence, and that evidence would in turn require evidence, and so on forever."

"Wait a minute." Sheridan says. "You're throwing that out there pretty quickly. Slow down."

"Well, let's take a closer look at how we define 'reason.' You've said that it's reasonable to doubt everything for which we don't have evidence. Let me offer another view of reason. Philosopher

Anthony Kenny has defined reason as the golden mean or optimal balance between doubt and belief. That means that the reasonable person doubts when it is appropriate to doubt and believes when it is appropriate to believe."

"Keep going," Sheridan says suspiciously.

"Sometimes doubt or skepticism is necessary, but that's only one side of reason. Think about it. The person who is completely skeptical about everything is a candidate for mental evaluation, not a paragon of reason."

"That seems a little harsh," Sheridan replies.

"Does it? Imagine somebody who was so skeptical that he refused to believe that he was awake, that there was an external world, or even that he existed. Would you seriously think that person was providing a model of the rational individual?"

"Maybe I would," Sheridan says with a wry smile.

"Well then you'd definitely be in the minority," I reply. "This notion that reason is found in doubt owes much to Descartes, the seventeenth-century Catholic philosopher who advocated that we test our beliefs with a systematic method of doubt. Obviously it's reasonable to doubt at times, but other times it's reasonable to believe, even though you could be wrong. Sometimes stepping out in faith is the most reasonable thing to do. That's what we do every morning when we get out of bed. We trust our sense perception to be reliable, we trust the world to be predictable, we trust people to be trustworthy. While we certainly don't want to be gullible, reason nonetheless often requires us to believe."

"Maybe you're wrong, Randal. Maybe being reasonable is much more demanding than you think. Maybe we should doubt everything."

"Okay," I reply, "just pause for a minute to look around." I give a broad wave of my hand at the flurry of activity in the Beatnik Bean: the afternoon sun streaming into the window, the crowds of students studying, writing, texting, talking and drinking a range of caffeinated beverages, the pleasant aromas of coffee and freshly baked pastries combining with the musty smell of old furniture, the hiss of espresso shots being pressed, the throaty idle of a delivery truck along with, for a few seconds, the deafeningly obnoxious roar of a passing Harley Davidson, the jangle of the doorbell as more patrons enter.

"Now tell me, Sheridan, as you take in all the sensory stimuli here in the Beatnik Bean, do you really think it's reasonable to doubt that you're here?"

By the look of his expression, it's clear that Sheridan is determined to follow through with the consequences of his skeptical view of reason. "Maybe I'm sleeping," he replies with a shrug. "How should I know?"

"So you're saying that you doubt that you're awake?" My eyes narrow as I look at him directly and say, "Okay, then pinch yourself. Hard."

Sheridan snickers in derision. "Who says pinching is the one sure-fire way to tell that you're dreaming? Are you telling me it's impossible to dream a pinch?" With that he waves a dismissive hand at me.

Now it's my turn to wear the skeptic's mantle. I look back to the espresso bar where one of the baristas is pouring water just off boil into a cup for an Americano. "Okay, how inclined are you to stick your hand in that cup to test whether you might be asleep?"

Suddenly Sheridan looks irritated. "Hey, I didn't say I was asleep. I said I don't know."

"Well, don't you want to find out?" I shoot back. "Look, you're not going to convince me that you doubt you're awake. And even if you did, you certainly wouldn't convince me that your doubt was the most rational position. The fact is that no rational person is a pure skeptic about everything, nor should they be. Even if you want to say that you doubt whether you're awake now, you sure didn't doubt the existence of the material world a few moments ago. In fact, you completely dismissed idealism without a second thought because it contradicted your commonsense beliefs about the world. And you were even more dismissive of solipsism. I agree with you. I don't consider idealism or solipsism remotely plausible. But I recognize that when I dismiss them I'm taking a step of faith—and so should you. Sorry, but you're living by faith whenever you believe you're awake and living in a material world."

Sheridan gives me a wicked grin. "Maybe I was just pretending to believe in a world and other minds for the sake of the argument. Maybe I'm just a figment of your imagination. Maybe I'm just a character in a story you've written, a mere literary pawn to make you rich and famous."

"Oh, now you've got it!" I say, laughing. "That's it!" I look over at you. "Sheridan is actually a character in a book I'm writing, right Reader?"

Sheridan grins. "I knew it! I just hope it's a good action novel. But I have a feeling, based on the lame topics of conversation, that it's actually a second-rate apologetics book."

"I don't know about second-rate," I reply. "Look, we can always spin out enormously implausible scenarios to explain the data of experience, but most of the time we don't do that—nor should we, because then we wouldn't believe anything. The fact is that day by day, moment by moment, in the vast majority of cases, we believe countless things without determinative evidence for them. As philosophers put it, we accept them as 'properly basic.' We trust our beliefs, and in most cases we're rational to do so."

I pause and then gesture at a premed student sitting on a stool in the window looking like a deer caught in the headlights as she flips through a massive anatomy textbook. "Nor do scientists suddenly set their faith commitments aside when they begin to do science. The best scientists believe the testimony of peer-reviewed research. They trust the vetting process of academic journals like *Scientific American* and the *New England Journal of Medicine*. They also trust their teachers and coworkers. They trust their scientific instruments. They trust their memory. And they ultimately trust the natural world to display the regularities of natural law. If scientists threw out trust and became across-the-board skeptics, then science would grind to a halt immediately."

After a suggestive pause, I add, "As I said, the man who doubts everything is the man headed for the insane asylum."

"Uh, just so you know, the term 'insane asylum' passed out of use several decades ago," Sheridan snarks.

"My mistake," I reply. "I meant to say 'loony bin.'" Sheridan gives me a withering glance. "The point is that once we recognize the essential place of belief in rationality, we'll be well on our way to a correct appraisal of the epistemic status of Christian belief. The dichotomy you're assuming between faith and reason just isn't there—belief is tangled up with both of them. Many so-called skeptics and free thinkers still take Mark Twain seriously when he defined faith as 'believing what you know ain't true.' You already borrowed Richard Dawkins's insulting term by calling me a 'faith-head'—as if Dawkins himself somehow doesn't exercise faith every day as a scientist and human being."

I lean forward a bit for emphasis. "Sheridan, the rational person is the one who exercises the proper amount of faith, not the one who eschews faith. So it's a little amusing to hear people say they believe only by reason and evidence. The atheist who insists that he exercises reason but not faith is like the child who insists that he breathes air but not oxygen. As long as you're breathing you're taking in oxygen, and as long as you're reasoning you're going on faith."

"So then can we just believe anything because it's all faith?"

"That's not what I'm saying," I reply, trying to suppress my exasperation, "but I do believe you're giving me more gray hair! Look, we have to recognize that faith is a starting point for reasoning. For instance, a scientist needs to trust sense perception. How can we ever confirm that our sense perception is reliable without drawing on our sense perception? We can't. We have to trust it."

"Sheesh," Sheridan sneers. "That's not true. I don't 'trust' my sense perception. I draw a reasonable conclusion that it must be reliable or I wouldn't be here. If my vision, hearing and touch weren't reliable, I never would've made it to the Beatnik Bean—I would have been flattened by a bus or fallen down a manhole. Evolution has given us adaptive beliefs that aid our survival. Adaptive beliefs are bound to be largely true or they wouldn't get passed on. So evolution has selected for survival those creatures that produce mostly true beliefs. And that's how I know what's true without faith."

"That might be true, but we can't know for sure. All sorts of false beliefs are adaptive, too, often more so than true beliefs. So we don't know that we didn't get to the Beatnik Bean on false but adaptive beliefs."

"What do you mean about adaptive false beliefs?"

"Okay," I say, "I may believe that I am the world's best singer. Even if I'm mediocre, the belief that I'm the next Frank Sinatra may give me the confidence to put on a better performance than I would have been capable of had I known the truth. So that'd be an adaptive false belief."

"That's one example," Sheridan says. "But how many beliefs are like that?"

"Quite a few, I think. I mean, we humans tend to think we're smarter, better looking and more athletic than others of equivalent intelligence, looks and fitness. But there's a real benefit to having these kinds of false beliefs. If we really were fully objective about ourselves, we would likely do worse in day-to-day activities.

"Anyway," I say, putting my hands in the small of my back and stretching, "I don't have to establish how many of our adaptive beliefs might be false. I just have to point out that you're making a leap by assuming that most of our adaptive beliefs are true. The bottom line is that the starting point of knowledge is faith. From the moment we take our first breath, everything we come to know is built on faith."

8

So Which Beliefs Are "Properly Basic"?

* * *

Sheridan holds up his hands in resignation. "Fine, it may be that we accept some beliefs without direct evidence, but that's only because we have to. We simply must assume that sense perception is trustworthy and that there's an external world and stuff like that. But you can't plausibly claim that we need to believe in your sky God to make sense of the world, because billions don't."

"I don't know about your criterion," I reply. "I don't think we accept certain beliefs as properly basic because of some universally perceived necessity. After all, idealists don't find belief in the external world necessary, so if that criterion were correct then we couldn't believe in the existence of the external world. You need to find another criterion to distinguish which beliefs require evidence and which don't."

Sheridan sits up straighter, saying, "Well, one criterion must be the real world versus the fictional world of religion. We all need to see and feel the ground to walk, but how do religious people learn stuff about their particular and contradictory gods? Through some sort of sixth sense that's not available to others?"

"I think that most of what a Christian would claim to know in a properly basic way would come through other familiar modes of properly basic belief, like the testimony of other human persons. In other cases we might perceive God in an immediate way, not unlike what we perceive through sense perception or reason."

"Hold on," Sheridan interrupts. "I perceive a sunset because I see a sunset. It's that simple."

"Sheridan, when you see a sunset you come to hold many beliefs that are natural and reasonable. You may believe 'I see a sunset' and 'the sun now looks orange.' But you also might come to believe that 'the sunset is beautiful.' That could also be, in my view, a very reasonable belief. If you can believe that it's beautiful, why couldn't you also believe that 'God made the sun' based on your perception of the sun setting? If you want to exclude beliefs about God, then I'd like to hear on what basis you do so."

"No problem, Randy. In the case of sense perception I directly see something. Not so for your mystical God-perception. I don't see a God making the sun set."

"You should be careful about assuming that all the ways we come to knowledge must pass through sense perception."

"I don't follow you."

"Well, our rational intuition of mathematical and logical truths doesn't function in the same way as sense perception. We don't learn the truths of algebra or calculus in the same way that we learn that it's raining outside. Those are different ways of knowing, and we recognize the autonomy of each. So why can't the perception of God have its own unique status—why can't it be a distinct way of knowing? If you say that the only way to know is through sense perception, then that's basically imposing a Procrustean bed on our ways of knowing."

Sheridan says, "Say what?"

"Procrustes was a character in Greek mythology who ran an

inn. Every evening he would invite weary travelers to come and sleep in one of his beds. Unbeknownst to the poor pilgrims, Procrustes always made sure that everybody fit his beds perfectly. If someone was too short, he would stretch their appendages, and if they were too tall he would amputate whatever wouldn't fit. The story of Procrustes and his bed has since become a metaphor for cases where a grid is forced onto data in a way that makes the data fit the grid."

Sheridan laughs. "Yeah, I remember this now. Isn't mythology great? Procrustes is almost as grisly as some Bible stories I've read! Look, let me be blunt: What separates your God beliefs from good old-fashioned magic? If you can believe that an invisible sky God made the sunset, then why can't I just believe that a giant pink dragon created the sunset? If you give up requiring people to defend their beliefs with evidence, it becomes a free-for-all where everyone can believe what they want."

"I take your pink dragon idea to be a form of *reductio ad absurdum*. That is, you're trying to argue against my view by claiming that it leads to absurd consequences. Thus, if I give up the obligation to provide evidence that God created the sunset then I have to accept the absurd consequence that another person could believe without evidence that a pink dragon created the sunset." Sheridan nods.

"Okay," I say, "I guess I don't have a problem conceding that. In principle it's possible that the belief that a pink dragon created the sunset could be properly basic. This shouldn't be too surprising, since all sorts of beliefs that appear to be extraordinary at first blush can be properly basic."

I look over my shoulder as if I'm about to share a big secret. "Did you know that some physics professors even tell their students that this rock-solid coffee table is composed of vibrating packets of energy in empty space? And their students believe them, too!"

Sheridan looks at me indignantly. "There's a crucial difference, Randal. You can test the physicist's claim to see if it's true. But beliefs about God can't be tested!"

"Wait, are you offering testability as a new criterion for determining which beliefs can be properly basic? How is an undergraduate supposed to test for him- or herself whatever a physics professor says about the world? They can't."

"Okay, that's tough," Sheridan admits, "but testability is still a virtue. If you hallucinate something in front of you, you could later test that perception to see if it's false—like if I think I see a goblin behind the coffee bar, I can go look more carefully, and ask the barista if he saw it and so on. But you can't test beliefs about a god, can you?"

I look surprised. "There are all sorts of beliefs that aren't testable in the narrow sense you're proposing but that are still excellent candidates for being properly basic sources of knowledge. The belief in the external world that we keep coming back to is a great example. We can't 'test' that. We assume it. And how can you test the claim that the world wasn't created five minutes ago with apparent age? How can you test the claim that you're not just a brain in a vat being fed sensory stimuli? There are innumerable things we believe that we can't test. So I don't know why you're singling out beliefs in God because they're not 'testable.'"

"The problem with religious people," Sheridan replies, "is that they're just not open to the evidence. They're not open to changing or reflecting on what they believe. You can't reason with them."

"Riiight," I say slowly, "so now the criterion is willingness to change one's beliefs? Pardon me for being skeptical, but you're fooling yourself if you think that an atheist like Richard Dawkins is any more open-minded when it comes to basic worldview issues than your average conservative Christian. I often hear atheists play up the claim that they're 'open to the evidence,' but in my experience they can be as intransigent and closed-minded as anybody. Religious people certainly don't have a monopoly on fundamentalism."

"It might look that way to you," Sheridan snaps back, "but that's just because we know what good evidence looks like and we can see that you don't have any. We're holding the royal flush and you're still trying to ante up with a pair of twos."

"That's just an assertion," I retort. "Anybody can say the same thing. I can assert that your evidence isn't good enough for me. That could simply be a way of hiding my stubborn intransigence behind a veil of rationality."

9

God Is Not a Hypothesis

* * *

Sheridan shakes his head in dismay. "So now a critical mind is a sign of 'stubborn intransigence'? Dude, is nothing sacred for you?"

"Since when have you started worrying about the sacred?" I grin. "Listen, Sheridan, I'd like to return to my other complaint with Vic Stenger's book *God: The Astonishing Hypothesis.*

"As I said, I disagree with the assumption that Christians need to justify their belief in God as a hypothetical posit that's supposed to explain some feature of their experience. Certainly one could argue for God in this way, but it's not the usual way Christians think about God. From the Christian perspective, God is not a hypothesis; rather, he's a lived reality. Atheists often assume that the only way to have a reasonable belief about God is if the existence of God is treated as a hypothesis that we reason to at the end of an argument, but from a Christian perspective that puts things backward."

"I can understand why you're not happy with treating belief in God as a hypothesis," Sheridan says. "If it were a hypothesis, you'd see how indefensible the belief really is. Even if I thought God was a defensible hypothesis, your belief in your particular Yahweh trinity certainly wouldn't be. Ockham's razor takes care of that."

"Actually, I think that's probably right," I reply. "If you think God is only a hypothesis, it's unlikely that you'll ever be able to justify a hypothesis sufficiently rich that it will look anything like the Christian doctrine of God. Under those conditions it's hardly surprising that God comes out looking 'astonishing' and 'unjustified.' So I readily admit that this hypothesis view might spell trouble for Christian belief.

"However," I add quickly, noticing Sheridan's *aha!* expression, "I don't think that Christians hold their beliefs in this way. They believe things about God with the same kind of immediacy that they hold beliefs about the existence of the external world and other minds. And if atheists really want to understand Christians, they need to get over the assumption that the only way to have reasonable beliefs or knowledge of God is by way of a hypothesis inference."

"Okay, dude, I get it. You don't think God is a hypothesis. But what is God, then? How about this: Do you think that God talks to Christians?" Sheridan begins to speak in a deep, sonorous voice. "Randal, today I've planned for you to meet a sinful atheist at the Beatnik Bean. Do your best to save him because otherwise I'm going to wallop him with a thunderbolt at 10:37 tonight."

"I think you're confused—Zeus is the one who uses thunderbolts. But I'm glad you raised the question of whether God speaks to people. Why is that impossible?"

Sheridan initially looks shocked, but his expression quickly changes to one of supreme disdain. "You ask why? Because that opens the floodgates, that's why. If you start saying that God talks to people then anybody can say God told them to do anything, like that cult leader who killed his whole flock with Kool-Aid."

"Not so fast," I reply. "What you believe God could possibly say depends on what kind of being you believe God to be. Based on what a Christian believes about God, there are many beliefs that can be rejected in principle as not having come from him."

"Oh yeah, like what?"

"One time a guy told me that he believed God wanted him to cheat on his wife. I felt confident telling him that God would never commend such an action."

Sheridan smirks. "So maybe it was actually the little devil sitting on his left shoulder who whispered that idea in his ear. Listen, I want you to be clear about what this speaking is, exactly. Are you saying people hear an audible voice? Or do they see an angelic apparition?"

"There are all sorts of ways God might speak to a person. Like I said before, he can speak through the testimony of another person. I believe I was speaking God's voice to that man when I told him God would never approve of him cheating."

Sheridan looks frustrated. "That just pushes the question back a notch. You and your friend obviously disagreed about God's will, so who settles those kinds of disputes? There's no World Court in The Hague to settle divine debates, is there?"

"Not exactly, but I think there's a significant body of evidence to provide guidance in these sorts of matters. For instance, it was easy for me to point this guy to the Bible, which he accepted as authoritative, and show him that God had already said things that falsified his claim."

After a pause to take a sip of coffee I continue. "God can also speak through an event. Let's say that Jerry and his troop of Boy Scouts get lost in the woods and he prays to God to show him the right way out. At that moment he sees the flash of a meteorite to his right, which he takes as a sign that he is to veer to the right. And sure enough, by turning in that direction he quickly leads the troop out of the woods. It seems to me that it would be very reasonable for Jerry to conclude that God spoke to him through the flash of the meteorite."

"So God speaks through rocks that burn up in the atmosphere, huh?" Sheridan leans over and knocks his forehead on the coffee table. Then without looking up he asks, "Do you believe that people can literally hear God speak like a human being or not?"

"If God exists, he is surely able to manipulate sound waves to sound like a human voice, so I don't discount that possibility. But it certainly is not the norm. God often speaks through prayer, the reading of Scripture and the testimony of others in the community."

"That's pretty vague. How does God speak through prayer, exactly?"

"Let's say that Jerry prays, asking God for direction to show him which person in his office needs to hear the gospel. Immediately Fred comes to mind, an accountant from the third floor whom Jerry barely knows. That could be God's answer to Jerry's prayer, though at this point Jerry may not be sure. But let's say that Jerry does venture to speak to Fred. Immediately Fred bursts into tears, confesses that his life is in shambles, and five minutes later becomes a Christian. At that point I think Jerry would have excellent grounds to believe that God had indeed directed him to speak to Fred."

"Awww, dude, come on, that's so hokey."

"No more so than other modes of justified belief—and don't forget that faith and evidentiary reason *both* had a role. My claim is that Christians can come to have a properly basic knowledge of God in much the way that we gain knowledge through other avenues such as sense perception, reason and testimony. I would contend that basic Christian beliefs like 'God loves me' and 'God was in Christ reconciling the world to himself' are properly basic."

"Sorry, Randal, I'm not convinced. If Christian beliefs really were, as you say, 'properly basic,' they would be more widely accepted—like the truths of reason that everyone can agree on."

"Wait a minute. Now you're proposing criteria for proper basicality again. This time you're saying that properly basic beliefs are those that are 'obvious to most people most of the time.' Is that criterion itself obvious to most people most of the time?"

"Dude, I wasn't stating any 'belief' or 'criterion,'" Sheridan says with irritation. "I was just pointing out why your claim that Christian beliefs can be properly basic doesn't work."

"But your objection is based on the assumption that properly basic beliefs must be obvious to most people most of the time. And yet you haven't provided any evidence that that very claim is obvious to most people most of the time. If it isn't—and let me be clear that I think it isn't—then you need an argument for it."

I'm not sure Sheridan follows the point, but neither does he look particularly interested in trying to. He waves his hand dismissively. "Okay, whatever. Forget about my so-called criterion for a moment. It strikes me as a plausible guide even if you don't like it. Just answer me this: What is it that makes your religious beliefs so that they don't require evidence?"

"Let's back up to sense perception again. You walk into the room and see an apple on the table. As a result you come to believe that 'there's an apple on the table.' That belief is justified for you not as the end of a long chain of reasoning but in a basic, immediate way, simply as you have the experience. Unless you have a reason to distrust your perception, you're justified in accepting it."

"And that 'reason not to'—that's what you've been calling a 'defeater'?"

"Precisely."

"So then what would a defeater of your sense perception look like?"

"There are all sorts of possibilities. So let's say I seem to see the apple. If I also know that Harold just slipped a hallucinogenic drug in my drink, then I will have a defeater for the belief that there's an apple on the table in front of me because I'll have a general reason to distrust everything my cognitive faculties seem to be reporting, at least until the effect of the drug has worn off."

Sheridan begins to nod in acknowledgment. "I think I get the idea. So if you're wearing red-tinted glasses, that would be a defeater for the belief that the apple you see is red because everything you see while wearing the glasses is red."

"That's right. I don't know why you dropped philosophy, Sheridan—you're a born philosopher. Your example would constitute an undercutting defeater because the revelation that you're wearing red glasses would undercut your ground to believe anything you see is red, including the apple. It still may be the case that the apple in front of you is red, but you would no longer have a reason to believe that it is. In that case you should be agnostic about the actual color of the apple until you take off the glasses. Maybe it's red and maybe it isn't."

I continue the thread of discussion by explaining, "While an undercutting defeater simply undermines your reasons to believe a proposition true, a rebutting defeater gives you grounds to believe it's false. Let's say that after you take off your red glasses the apple looks yellow. Now you not only lack a reason to believe the apple is red. You also have a reason to believe it's not red. The yellow appearance constitutes a rebutting defeater for the claim that the apple is red."

"Do you have an example that doesn't involve fruit?"

"Okay, say you're in Vegas. While in attendance at a magic show you seem to see somebody sawed in half. If you think about it, you have two defeaters for the belief that a person really was sawed in half. First off, you have an undercutting defeater for the belief based on the very fact that you're at a magic show and thus you know not to trust your senses. In addition, you have a rebutting defeater based on your background knowledge that people who are cut in half die and the lady on stage looks perfectly comfortable as she waves at the audience.

"As these defeaters illustrate, although sense perception is generally reliable, it can mislead. New evidence can arise that leads us to reject our justification for a sense perception. We trust our sense perception unless and until we have a reason to doubt it.

My thesis is that at least some Christian beliefs like 'God loves me' can be properly basic for the person who has them. That is, so long as there are no undercutting defeaters or rebutting defeaters, a person is warranted in accepting basic beliefs about God just as they accept basic beliefs about the natural world."

A glimmer of recognition enters Sheridan's eye. "I follow what you're saying when it comes to sense perception. But as for your religious beliefs, it still looks like you're just trying to find a way to get off the hook from defending them. After all, aren't there plenty of defeaters to the idea of an all-powerful and loving God?"

"Just consider the parallel case. When Albert prays, he senses strongly that God loves him. As a result, he comes to believe 'God loves me' with the same immediacy that we come to believe 'the apple is red.' My argument is that absent defeaters, 'God loves me' and other beliefs about God can be properly basic for Albert just like the beliefs of sense perception."

Sheridan looks completely incredulous. "But that assumes that God exists, doesn't it? It's circular. Dude, that's a complete crock!"

"Well, obviously God must exist and love Albert for Albert to be able to know 'God loves me.' That much is true. But I'm saying that whether God exists or not, Albert's belief that God loves him can be justified so long as there are no defeaters to it."

Sheridan shakes his head. "Weird."

"No, it's not weird. It's just like our knowledge of the external world. If the external world exists, then we can have knowledge of it. But even if the idealist is ultimately correct and there is no external world of substance corresponding to our sense perceptions, it's still rational to believe that there is. I see no reason why the same thing can't be true for beliefs about God."

Sheridan crosses his arms in mystified defiance. Unsatisfied by his intransigence, I persist. "What's the problem? Why can't Albert's knowledge of God be immediate, just like his knowledge of the world? Why isn't that belief justified?"

"Because we have a scientific account of how you physically perceive a physical object, and religion is different! Light waves hit a piece of fruit and then strike the eye and produce a visual picture in the mind. But there is no analogy here with God, unless you're claiming that God is some object that can be sensed."

"Sheridan, you seem very forgiving when it comes to your so-called purely scientific understanding of sense perception."

Sheridan looks at me curiously. "Forgiving?"

"You forgive, or just ignore, the huge gaps in our understanding of how sense perception actually functions. Basically, the account you just gave moves from light hitting the eye to getting a 'visual picture in the mind.' But what's the link between photons hitting the rods and cones in our eye and our having a mental image of an external reality? Can you explain how those are linked? If you're going to restrict properly basic beliefs only to those beliefs that come to us through 'non-mysterious' processes, then vision won't qualify since philosophers still have no workable theory of how we move from light waves to vision. And that's to say nothing of even more mysterious modes of perception like proprioception."

"Pro-what?"

"That's the way we sense the boundaries and spatial location of our own bodies. There's probably no dimension of perception more fundamental, and more perplexing, than that. How do you know where your hands and feet are at any given moment? The answer is that you proprioceive them. But how do you do that? What proprioception actually is, and how it works, remains a mystery. So are you saying that we're not justified in holding beliefs about the boundaries and location of our bodies because we don't have an account of this type of knowledge?"

"I'm still not convinced, man—I mean, my hands and feet are right here in front of me, but your sky God just isn't."

"Where your hands and feet are isn't the only problem. What about rational intuition? Most people agree that mathematics is among the most secure forms of knowledge since it comes from pure reasoning. You said always believe the mathematician, right?"

"Yup—and hardly any mathematicians are Christians!"

"I don't know about that, but rational intuition is no less mysterious than sense perception. We don't bump into anything when we perceive abstract mathematical numbers and relationships; we intuit something. And yet what intuition is, how it works, and what it is that we are actually grasping—those are all mysteries. This type of knowledge provides a profound puzzle, as the eminent atheistic philosopher Colin McGinn admits."

I reach into my trusty bag and pull out McGinn's *Problems in Philosophy*. "Here's how McGinn puts it: 'Let us candidly admit that a priori knowledge confutes dogmatic naturalism: it does indeed call for the attribution of non-natural mental faculties, capable of reaching out beyond space and the causal order. As divine revelation acquaints us with God, so the abstract world is revealed to us by miraculous methods.'[5]

"Did you hear the parallel he draws? Reason is as miraculous as divine revelation. So here's the problem. If you reject the idea that we can perceive truths about God because such perception is mysterious, then you likewise must reject the deliverances of rational intuition like seven plus five equals twelve and sense perceptions like 'I see a red apple' because these basic modes of knowledge are also mysterious."

"All your lecturing is giving me flashbacks from philosophy class, and I think I'm finally figuring out the way you argue, Randal. You depend on the *tu quoque*. That's a fallacy, dude, and you seem to have mastered it."

"Ooh, nice—going Latin on me, eh? So you think I'm defending everything I think by trying to point out that you think in the same way? And you don't like that?"

"Exactly! Instead of defending your indefensible beliefs, you're trying to attack mine with my own arguments—even though what I think is the current pinnacle of advanced, scientific thought and what you think is a two-thousand-year-old myth. We do not think and believe the same things in the same way."

"But Sheridan, often the *tu quoque*—the 'you also'—is a completely legitimate rebuttal. Let's say that Paul is looking for a way to get Fred's old uninsured Trans-Am out of their condo's parking lot. So he presents a proposal to the condo board that all uninsured vehicles on the grounds should be removed. The only problem is that in his excitement Paul has forgotten that he has an uninsured Winnebago parked on the other side of the building. Surely it would be perfectly appropriate for Fred to point out that if Paul insists on pushing through his amendment it will force the removal of his Winnebago as well. That's a legitimate example of the *tu quoque*."

I resettle myself in my chair and continue. "Sheridan, you're basically like Paul—trying to get my Trans-Am removed from the parking lot. And I keep pointing out that if you insist on that it will require the removal of your Winnebago as well. That's a fair point to make, isn't it?"

10

How to Show That
"God Loves Me" Is False

★ ★ ★

Okay," Sheridan says, "let me shift the ground of my objection. The idea of defeaters makes good sense in the case of sense perception. I may believe there's an apple on the table but further inquiry can prove me wrong. No problem. But what kind of defeaters could possibly dislodge any of Albert's beliefs about God?"

"Actually," I reply, "Christian beliefs are, for the most part, eminently falsifiable."

"Oh, really? How so?"

"Start with the resurrection of Jesus. The way to falsify that belief is straightforward: just produce the body."

"Oh, very convenient, Randal. Your example is a belief about an event that is lost in the mists of antiquity. The body of Jesus would have decayed long ago, if he ever existed to begin with. You know the resurrection is by now safely beyond falsification."

"I'll admit that it's unlikely that evidence would arise that would undermine the resurrection, but that's not to say it's impossible. It's perfectly conceivable that an archaeologist could recover the bones of Jesus in a tomb along with documentary evidence that the resurrection was a hoax staged by the apostles. That kind of evidence would most certainly disconfirm the resurrection."

"But how about Albert's belief that God loves him? How are you going to falsify that one?"

"There are all sorts of ways you could falsify a belief like that."

"Cool. You got my attention."

"Let's say you present an argument that God does not exist. To the extent that your argument is a persuasive defeater to the belief that God exists, it's also a defeater of the belief that 'God loves Albert' since non-existent entities don't love anything."

Sheridan leans forward eagerly. "So what are your arguments for God's non-existence?"

"Atheists have been developing them for hundreds of years: the problem of evil, the impossibility of a perfect being, the problem of religious diversity and so on. You can check out the literature for yourself. I'm not doing your work for you."

"But obviously those arguments are going to fail since you can't prove a negative," says Sheridan. "You can't prove that something doesn't exist. I may have only seen black and white swans but I can't prove there are no purple swans. Ergo, you can't prove there is no God."

"I hear that claim from atheists a lot these days, but it's just not true. You certainly can prove that something doesn't exist. The strongest way would be by showing that the concept of the entity in question is incoherent, because if something is incoherent then it can't exist. For example, by definition you know there can't be a square circle because the concept of circle is incompatible with the property of being square. Many critics of Christianity have attempted this kind of argument. For example, some have argued that the Trinity is incoherent: just as a circle cannot be square so one God cannot be three divine persons. Others have argued that there is a conflict between divine attributes like omnipotence and perfect goodness."

"No argument there from me—it's a proven fact!"

"Yes, those critics insist that if God really is all-powerful, then he must be able to do evil actions. But if he can do evil then he cannot be perfectly good. So it would seem that God can't be both omnipotent and perfectly good. I may not find these arguments persuasive, but the fact remains that in principle you could provide a rebutting defeater for the claim that 'God loves Albert' by showing that God, as defined by the Christian, doesn't exist."

"All right, anything else?"

"Well, here's an undercutting defeater. Freud argued that belief in a loving heavenly father is generated by wish fulfillment. That is, we project a loving heavenly father onto a cold, hostile universe because we can't handle reality. If it can be shown that belief in God is a psychological projection, that would provide an undercutting defeater: that is, even if God exists, we would have lost our reason to think he does. And again, if Albert loses his reason to think God exists, then neither should he believe that God loves him."

Sheridan nods thoughtfully. "I think I'm getting the idea."

"So since beliefs like 'God loves Albert' are in principle vulnerable to rebutting and undercutting defeaters, the skeptic cannot plausibly dismiss these beliefs as being unfalsifiable. But then if these beliefs are in principle falsifiable, then the skeptic has an evidential burden to show that they are, in fact, false. He can't simply dismiss the task as a fool's errand. Atheists don't get to dismiss their cake and eat it, too."

Sheridan starts laughing and slaps the coffee table. "This is hilarious! I've got you trying to defend Christianity by laying out the case to show it's false!"

Then he turns serious. "But you're not really showing that. All your 'defeaters' may sound good, but they don't really mean anything because whenever one pops up you can just change your beliefs to suit it. Christianity is like an amorphous blob that swallows up every objection and just keeps rolling along, always changing like a chameleon."

I nod. "Ah, the invisible gardener."

"Invisible what?"

"Antony Flew famously objected to belief in God by comparing it to belief in an invisible gardener. Here's the picture. You walk into a forest clearing and your friend says that the clearing is tended by a gardener. You fail to see any evidence of this and so you suggest that the two of you wait for this mysterious gardener to show up. But no gardener ever appears. You reasonably expect your friend to admit defeat and give up belief in his gardener, but instead he modifies the belief by saying that the gardener did visit the clearing, and the reason you didn't see him is because he happens to be invisible."

Sheridan chuckles. "Oh, right. This is starting to sound familiar."

"Well, you're not that easily deterred so you enclose the clearing in an electric fence to ensure that you will detect this mysterious gardener should he visit again. When nothing disturbs the fence your friend has an answer to this too: the invisible gardener can also pass through fences. Pretty soon it becomes clear. You cannot really falsify your friend's belief in this gardener because whatever new evidence against it may arise, he'll just adjust his belief accordingly."

Sheridan nods with approval. "Yeah, that sounds like God belief all right. That's why it's so frustrating talking with you theologians—apologetics is just a matter of painting the bull's eye around the arrow!"

"Maybe if you're talking about fringe beliefs or cult leaders, but that simply isn't true when talking about historic, orthodox Christianity. If you assume a set of definitional claims about God, like his triune identity and a particular set of attributes, then your belief is not a mere cipher. It has real content and can be falsified."

"Yeah, but if your 'standard definitions' fail you can always adopt new ones. Look at the way God evolved from a humanlike demigod walking in a garden to the lofty deity of Christian theology. Don't try to tell me that the God in the Old Testament is the same as the God American Christians pray to for parking spots. Look, imagine if Christians finally came to realize that a basic doctrine in their theology is indefensible. Do you really think they'd reject Christianity? Of course not! They'll just drop that doctrine and shift all the others. The fact is that the Christianity of today shares no substantial identity with the Christianity of medieval Europe or the Roman Empire, not to mention the Jewish religion of the Old Testament."

"I disagree with that, Sheridan."

Sheridan throws up his hands. "Of course you disagree."

"Seriously, I think you're focusing on non-essential changes. Consider the practice of medicine as an analogy. There's no doubt that medicine has changed enormously from the ancient Greek world of Hippocrates to the modern treatments available at the Mayo Clinic. And yet Hippocrates and those Mayo clinicians are agreed on maintaining the Hippocratic Oath to do no harm. That is a basic unity. Despite all its diversity through time, Christianity has a similar kind of underlying unity."

"And that is . . . ?"

"To begin with, the conviction that God sent his Son to offer a fallen world the way to reconciliation."

"That's what you say, Randal, but many Christians would disagree with you."

"Unfortunately, Sheridan, I'm going to have to pull out the old *tu quoque* once again. If your objection applies to me, it applies to you as well. Consider scientific theories. They can always be changed, expanded, amended to accommodate new data. Theories aren't abandoned because they're falsified in a simple, straightforward sense. Rather, they're abandoned because they become no longer useful. But for a long time a theory can be sustained in the teeth of contradictory evidence through successive emendations. So whatever Christian theologians may do in their theories is, in principle, nothing different from what scientists do in their theories."

"But your beliefs about God are private. That's not like science or even sense perception. If I think I see an apple on the table, I can call a buddy of mine and ask for confirmation. But you can have a Christian and a Muslim look at the same sunset and draw two completely different conclusions. One says it is the handiwork of Jesus while the other says it's from Allah."

"Sure, and the atheist looks at the same sunset and says none of the above," I add. "We all disagree. But again, that's not anything unique to religion, Sheridan. Stephen Crane's *The Red Badge of Courage* is a classic of American literature; that much is agreed upon. But critics are absolutely divided on its interpretation. Some see it as an inspiring depiction of the way war forges cowardly boys into courageous men, while others argue that it's a profound deconstruction of the ideology of war and heroism. Exact same data, completely different interpretations."

I cross my legs. "The same fundamental disagreements characterize scientific inquiry. Two competing theories present two completely different ways to interpret the same data. That's as much your reality as it is mine."

11

The Swedish Atheist
and the Scuba Diver

* * *

Randal, I must admit that I have a certain morbid fascination with all the ingenuity you exert in desperately propping up your belief system," Sheridan says. "But the bottom line is that you argue the way you do because you were raised a Christian. Things would be different if you were born in India or Saudi Arabia."

"Sure, and they would be for you too! I see we're back to your geographic objection. You're claiming that I'm a Christian because I was raised in a Christian home in a Christian culture and therefore that Christianity is false. But that doesn't follow. Even if I believed Christianity due to social conditioning, it still might be true."

"Yeah, but if you accept Christianity only because of the way you were raised then you don't have a reason to be a Christian, right? That'd be like your undercutting defeater."

"That's fair. If that was the only reason I were a Christian then I might lose my grounds for being one. But I don't believe my up-bringing exhausts my reasons for being a Christian, so your point isn't really relevant. I certainly agree that we ought to think through the inherited assumptions of our culture. The Baptists who were raised in the Bible-belt Christian culture need to challenge themselves to think critically and objectively about those beliefs. But the same goes for atheists raised in an atheistic culture."

Sheridan looks indignant. "What are you talking about? Atheists have no culture."

"Come on, Sheridan, that's way too harsh. I once met an atheist who appreciated opera."

Sheridan rolls his eyes. "Lame joke, dude. But seriously, atheists don't have the cultural institutions and sacred texts and rituals of religious culture that you do. We're free of that kind of baggage."

"Really? So let me get this straight. I'm laden with chains of dogma while your vision is absolutely unimpeded?"

Sheridan nods. "That sounds about right."

I pause to contemplate whether to shine a spotlight on Sheridan's own baggage. But that seems a bit too personal this early in the conversation. So instead I decide to aim wider. "Consider a country like Sweden, one of the most skeptical and secular countries in the world," I say. "Sweden is dominated by people who are atheists and institutions that reinforce that atheism. The geographic distribution of atheism among residents of Sweden is not different from, say, the geographic distribution of Mormonism among residents of Utah or Christianity among residents of Kentucky. So if you claim that my beliefs are in doubt because I was born into a supposedly Christian nation, then the Swedish atheist's beliefs are suspect for much the same reason."

"I can see why you think that an atheist born into a secular country like Sweden should think through why they believe what they believe. But their position is characterized by doubting religion—so are you asking them to doubt their doubts?"

"Is that such a bad idea?" I retort.

"Wait a minute, Randy. If I'm supposed to doubt my doubt, I'd probably have to do it from the point of view of faith in one of the religions. So which one is it? Maybe the Hare Krishnas? Should I shave my head and hand out flowers at the airport?"

"I don't think Hare Krishnas do that anymore."

"Then what? Should I go kosher like an orthodox Jew, or be baptized and join a Christian church? Which religion do you expect me to adopt in order to test my atheism?"

"A real objectivity test doesn't require us to adopt another set of beliefs. It just requires us to adopt the same critical perspective toward our beliefs that somebody who didn't hold them would take. And in principle anybody can do that. Since the Swedish atheist can suspend and scrutinize his beliefs as surely as anybody else, the Swedish atheist should take the outsider test as surely as the Utah Mormon or the Kentucky Baptist."

"But not just Swedish atheists, right?"

"Well, why would you limit the obligation to Swedes?" I retort. "What about atheists who are raised in Oregon? That's a highly secular state. So should they also consider an outsider test for their beliefs?"

"Maybe."

"Okay, but what about the atheist who was raised in a Christian society? What about an atheist who is raised in the Bible belt of Tulsa, Oklahoma, by atheist parents? Does she get exempted from examining her beliefs because she grew up in a largely Christian population? Isn't it still wholly possible that she could have been indoctrinated as surely as her Christian neighbors?"

Sheridan shrugs. "Sure, it's possible. But it'd be a lot more likely if her parents were Baptists. So the Baptist kid has a bigger obligation to think through her beliefs."

"That's just silly. If Muslims and Christians can trace their faith to their upbringing and life circumstances, then atheists can as well. The fact is that we all have to examine our commitments objectively and critically. Some people might be Christians because of a Christian upbringing. Others may be atheists because of an atheist upbringing. And of course some people are atheists because of a Christian upbringing."

Sheridan looks interested. "Come again?"

"Have you heard of Fred Phelps?"

Sheridan shrugs noncommittally. "Nope."

"He's the infamous pastor of a small Kansas church that runs the website Godhatesfags.com."

Sheridan's expression darkens. "Oh yeah. Those guys."

"Apparently Phelps believes that pretty much everybody but his congregation is going to hell. And as you can guess, he especially hates homosexuals. With all that hatred and intolerance, is it any surprise that his son Nate Phelps ended up as an outspoken atheist?"

"Isn't it a bit condescending to suggest that the son is an atheist simply because his dad is an idiot? Sure his dad may have helped him along, but this guy could have all sorts of intellectual reasons to be an atheist."

"So you think that Christians all hold their beliefs because of social factors but that it's 'condescending' to suggest that atheists hold their beliefs based on social factors? Social factors shape all our beliefs. And we all need to be highly aware of those factors as we assess the strength of the evidence for our beliefs."

"Aren't you just trying to avoid your own obligations for self-reflection by putting the spotlight on others?"

"Hey, I'm not asking for special exemptions," I say. "I think all people should strive to be objective and fair thinkers, critical in their beliefs and generous in assessing the beliefs of others. In other words, I don't think that we should seek a one-off test to examine our beliefs. Instead, we should strive to develop intellectual virtues in all the things we believe. There's a real danger with thinking that you just need a single test of whatever religious commitments you may hold and then somehow you're okay. Being a rational, fair thinker—that's a life's work."

Sheridan looks like he is beginning to drift away, so I switch to an illustration. "Back when I was in university I got my PADI license for scuba diving."

With that Sheridan suddenly snaps back to attention. "Scuba diving, huh? That's cool."

"Yeah, I was certified back in 1995 and I went on a few dives, but I haven't dived since. Now here's the crazy thing: When I received my PADI license, I was certified for life. So even though I cannot presently remember a thing about diving, I can still legally take my license into any dive shop around the world and rent scuba gear. The certification of my scuba diving skills in 1995 was at best only a reliable indicator of my skill for the following few months. It says nothing about my abilities now. That's what worries me about posing a single 'outsider' test for belief. It implies that if you pass this one test of belief then you're done and now you can go forth and shine your glowing rational countenance on the shadowy realms of irrational religion!"

With that flourish, a few people at nearby tables look over at us curiously. I lower my voice as I continue: "This outsider test you keep pushing reminds me of my PADI license. Just as the PADI certification equips you to scuba dive today, so the outsider test might equip you to believe responsibly today. But what about tomorrow? Next year? Next decade? If you've already been granted your lifetime certified rationality card, what will call you to account if your beliefs change? I wonder how many self-assured secularists were critical at one time but have since fallen into irrational intransigence, much like I lost the ability to dive."

Sheridan shakes his head, bemused. "Why don't you light a candle in the darkness? If you don't like the outsider test of religion, then what rational challenge do you propose instead to test belief?"

"As I've said, my solution is simple and fair. We all ought to strive for intellectual virtues like fairness, objectivity and open-mindedness. Not just in a single test of a single subset of beliefs, but rather in all our beliefs all the time. We need to wake up in the morning and say to ourselves, 'I'm going to be fair, objective and open-minded in my beliefs today!' All of us—scuba divers and Swedish atheists alike—need to keep reminding ourselves that belief, like life itself, is a long journey that requires constant adjustment. And if you demand that I question my beliefs without questioning your own, Sheridan, well, that's an indefensible double standard that just isn't reasonable."

12

Will the Real Atheist Please Stand Up?

★ ★ ★

I continue, "My Christian beliefs have been on the defensive for a while now. Not that I'm complaining, mind you. I'm a big boy. I can take it. But I wouldn't mind spinning the spotlight around for a bit. I'd really like to know why you hold your beliefs. Why is it that you're an atheist? What led you to draw that conclusion? After all, that too is a claim. You believe that God does not exist. And that belief is as much up for critical analysis as the belief that he does."

Sheridan mimics a buzzer sound from a game show: "Bzzzzt! Wrong, dude. I don't believe there is no God. *A-theist*. That means without belief in God."

I look at Sheridan strangely. "So you're saying that you don't actually believe the proposition 'God does not exist'?"

"Look, I'm not saying that I can prove there is no God."

"I didn't say anything about proof. There are all sorts of things I can't prove that I still believe. I've already noted many of them, including the belief that our sense perception is reliable and that matter exists. We can't prove these propositions, but we certainly believe them."

"Well, I'm without belief. I don't believe there is a God and I don't believe there isn't either. That's what I mean by atheist. I'm without belief either way."

"Sheridan, I don't want to be nit-picky here."

I can't stop myself from smiling a bit after I say that, and luckily Sheridan cracks a wry smile as well. I continue, "Okay, maybe I'll pick a few nits. What you're describing is actually agnosticism, the state of not knowing, or not having a firm belief, about whether God exists or not. That's not atheism. And frankly it makes me wonder whether you're trying to have the shock and awe of calling yourself an atheist without having the intellectual firepower to back it up. You're an 'atheist' when you're critiquing my beliefs or mocking a preacher you see on a street corner, but then the second we shift the spotlight onto you, suddenly—poof!—you're an agnostic."

Sheridan looks insulted. "Poof?" he retorts indignantly. "What do you mean 'poof'? Like I said, atheist is *ah-theist*. Without belief in God. I'll keep repeating that if you really insist."

"You're saying that an individual is an atheist if that individual lacks belief either in the existence of God or the nonexistence of God?"

"That's right."

"But that cannot be right, Sheridan," I reply earnestly. "If lack of belief in God is sufficient to be an atheist, then my dog Maggie is an atheist since she also lacks belief in God. Perhaps you think it's a bonus to recruit the animal kingdom to your side, but this strikes me as just plain silly—not to mention changing the definition of a pretty important word!"

"What's the big problem? Maybe atheism happens to be the default position for dogs, too. The 'null hypothesis' says that we should opt for non-intelligent explanations of phenomena unless we have a reason to do otherwise. That's the default view. And that's all I'm suggesting here. Atheism is the default view of the animal kingdom, including your pooch. Sorry, dude, but maybe all dogs don't go to heaven."

"You're misappropriating the null hypothesis," I reply. "The scientist may grant non-intelligent causal explanations a default position, but you can't seriously suggest that my dog accepts non-intelligent causal explanations by default. My Maltese has one thing on her mind: 'Where's my rawhide bone?' She doesn't have any opinion about whether God exists, nor is she able to. All you're doing is trivializing what it means to be an atheist. In your view even my pet rock would qualify as an atheist!"

"You have a pet rock?" Sheridan laughs. "Did you find it on eBay?"

"No, it's a treasured family heirloom. But enough about my pet rock. Here's another problem. You claim that lack of belief in God is sufficient to make one an atheist. That claim presumably depends on the general principle that if a person refuses to accept a proposition, then that person de facto accepts the negation of that proposition."

Sheridan nods cautiously, trying to figure out where I'm going with this. I continue, "So then by parity of reasoning it would follow that lack of belief in the non-existence of God would be sufficient to make one a theist. And that would mean that an agnostic would simultaneously qualify as an atheist and a theist."

Sheridan waves his hand dismissively. "Whatever, Randal. More philosophical tricks."

"No, I'm showing that the way you're defining the term *atheism* has absurd consequences. But if you don't care for my analysis, how about I just quote the definitions for *atheism* and *agnosticism* from the *Oxford Companion to Philosophy*? It's a standard reference work in the field."

"If it makes you feel good, go ahead," Sheridan says with noticeable disinterest. I reach into my book bag. As I pull out the thick volume, Sheridan sits up and exclaims, "Dude, this is hardly a fair fight when you're toting around a research library. Seriously, how many books do you have in your bag?"

"Apparently all the right ones," I reply with a mischievous grin. I open the book and leaf through the pages until I arrive at the entry under "atheism and agnosticism." I clear my throat to add a bit of pomp and circumstance and begin to read in my best Oxbridge accent (after all, it is the *Oxford Companion*):

> Atheism is ostensibly the doctrine that there is no God. Some atheists support this claim by arguments. But these arguments are usually directed against the Christian concept of God, and are largely irrelevant to other possible gods. Thus much Western atheism may be better understood as the doctrine that the Christian God does not exist.
>
> Agnosticism may be strictly personal and confessional— 'I have no firm belief about God'—or it may be the more ambitious claim that no one ought to have a positive belief for or against the divine existence.[6]

"Given that these are the standard definitions, I recommend you take note of them," I tell Sheridan. "According to our trusty *Oxford Companion*, if you have no belief about whether God exists or not, you're an agnostic, not an atheist."

Sheridan looks incredulous. "But in order to be an atheist on that definition I'd have to have an argument against any possible divine being. Nobody could do that, so by this definition nobody could be an atheist."

"Not true, Sheridan. As the definition makes clear, historically most of those who have designated themselves as 'atheists' have rejected the Judeo-Christian concept of God—that is, they believed it to be false. Philosophers and theologians refer to this Judeo-Christian concept as classical theism. In this view God is a bodiless, necessarily existent agent who is omnipotent, omniscient, omnipresent and perfectly good. So in the past, an atheist has been a person who denied the existence of the God of classical theism. I'd like to know whether you are an atheist in that sense."

"It's interesting that you don't mention the Trinity in that definition," Sheridan replies. "I thought that was pretty important to being a Christian, too."

"Sure, that's also essential to the Christian description of God. That just shows that even if the definition of God in classical theism is necessary for a Christian understanding of God, it's not sufficient. You're an agnostic about God as defined by classical theism, right?"

Sheridan gives a terse reply: "I am simply without belief in God the same way you're without belief in Zeus."

"I don't know about that. I'm happy to defend the position that Zeus does not exist. But you said you don't hold a belief either way concerning the existence of God as defined by classical theism."

Sheridan looks interested in my impiety concerning Zeus. "So how do you intend to defend the claim that Zeus does not exist?"

"The starting point is that the existence of Zeus is incompatible with the set of claims I do hold, claims I believe I'm justified in holding. But before getting pulled too far into what I believe and don't believe about Zeus, I really want to stay focused on what you believe and don't believe about the God of Christian theism."

"Hey, I'm right here, buddy. Ask away. Setting up pins and knocking them down."

"Okay, I'd like to get more clarity on the kind of agnostic you are. Our definition gives two types, the agnostic who says, 'I don't know' and the one who says, 'Nobody can know.' To illustrate, consider this statement: Tom Jones's single 'What's New, Pussycat?' sold more copies than the Beach Boys' single 'Surfer Girl.'"

"Tom Jones? The Beach Boys? Is there even anyone alive who knows who they are?"

"Funny, Sheridan. If I felt obliged to keep all my illustrations up-to-date then I'd be forever updating them. So I'll stick with Tom Jones and the Beach Boys. Now I have no opinion about whether that proposition is true or not, so I withhold belief in it. There's nothing controversial about that. I'm just admitting my ignorance. But it would be altogether a different thing if I were to claim that nobody could know whether the Tom Jones single sold more than the Beach Boys. That'd be presumptuous enough to require a defense on my part. So my question is whether your agnosticism is simply a commentary on your personal ignorance concerning God's existence or whether you are making the much more robust and controversial claim that nobody can know whether God exists."

"I'm just saying that I'm without belief in God," Sheridan says.

"Whew, that's a relief! Because if you were going to claim that nobody could know whether God exists or not, I'd definitely want to see an argument. But if you're just stating your own ignorance of the matter—well, that sure isn't atheism. Henceforth I dub thee—" I switch back to my English accent—"Sir Sheridan the Agnostic."

"Har. Dee. Har. Look, the main point is the same," Sheridan snaps. "None of us buy what you're selling."

"Ignoring for the moment the one-third of the planet alive now to whom your statement doesn't apply, that still raises the question of why. When it comes to the question of whether Tom Jones outsold the Beach Boys, I'm agnostic simply because I haven't looked into the matter. Is that the case for your agnosticism on the Christian God? Is it that you just haven't looked into the matter?"

"No, I have looked into it. I was forced to go to church for years and I know that it's all a big crock."

"Okay, now we're getting somewhere. I'd like to hear why you think you know it's a 'big crock.' What have you discovered that makes you an agnostic on the existence of the Christian God?"

"Why? I'm not trying to 'defend' anything here. My claim is simply that I am without belief in any gods. I don't believe in gods of any kind."

"But you just made a knowledge claim. It seems like we're going in circles here."

13

I Just Happen to Believe in
One Less God Than You

* * *

Sheridan looks at me directly. "Why am I without belief in God? It's simple, really. I see no reason to believe there is a God. I'm sure you're without belief that there's a rock on Pluto shaped like the Statue of Liberty. And that's because you find no reason to think there's a Statue-of-Liberty-shaped rock. That's just the way I am with God. Look, Randal, there's not such a big gap between you and me. I just happen to believe in one less god than you."

"I've heard that line before," I reply. "You're assuming that you can take God out of the picture and everything else stays the same. But that's just not true. If you really are an atheist, you end up rejecting not just God but all sorts of other things as well."

"Some of them gladly, like tithing!"

"If you're like other atheists I know, you reject a lot more than that, Sheridan. For instance, what's your view of angels and souls?"

"Angels? No, sorry, I live in the twenty-first century. The only angel I believe in is my girlfriend."

I decide not to acknowledge that cheesy quip, even though it probably plays better to her than to me. "Now are you merely without belief in angels and souls, or do you believe there are no angels or souls?"

Sheridan retorts, "Do you believe there are leprechauns and pixies living in the woods?"

"No, Sheridan, I don't. So do you believe there are no angels?"

"Sure, in the same way that you believe there are no leprechauns and pixies."

"I believe there are no leprechauns and pixies because those are characters of mythology and there's no evidence for them."

Sheridan smiles with satisfaction. "Ditto for angels."

"Certainly angels can be found in mythology," I reply, "complete with wings and harps. But that doesn't mean that the basic idea of an angel as a non-physical agent is merely mythological. Lions and wolves can also be found in mythology, but that doesn't mean that they don't also exist in reality."

"You seem sensitive about this, Randal," Sheridan says with a snicker. He dons a look of mock seriousness. "Dude, have you been 'touched by an angel'?"

"Just my wife," I reply.

"Touché," Sheridan says.

"And you don't believe in souls either, right?" I press on.

"No, I don't believe in souls because everything about human beings can be explained by appeal to the brain."

"Okay, Sheridan. What reason do you have to think that everything is explained by the brain?"

"Because science keeps closing gaps in our understanding. We may have needed the idea of a soul that animates the body when we thought the brain was just there to cool the blood. But now we know that thought, memory, agency, personal identity, emotion—everything's located in the brain. If you damage the brain you change the person. If you destroy the brain you lose the person. No souls need apply."

I scratch my head, puzzled. "The growth of our knowledge of the brain certainly shows that there's an intimate relationship between brain and mind; there's no doubt about that. But it's a leap to go from this intimate-dependence relationship to the conclusion that the mind is only the brain."

Sheridan crosses his arms. "And why would that be a 'leap,' exactly?"

"Let's start with Mr. Dreadlocks over there." Over on the couch by the fire we see a young man about twenty years old with dreadlocks and a nose ring just sitting down with a frothy cappuccino. As he sips, a pleased expression crosses his face. I turn to Sheridan. "Imagine that a pious Mormon neuroscientist who's never had so much as a sip of coffee devotes his research to studying Mr. Dreadlocks's brain states when he drinks espresso. After much research, the neuroscientist becomes a world expert on the brain states that accompany the drinking of espresso. He knows how the patterns of neuron synapses that accompany drinking an Americano differ from those that accompany drinking a cappuccino. He can even tell the differences in brain states between a person drinking regular espresso and organic espresso—and even single-origin organic espresso from Ethiopia!"

Sheridan whistles. "That's pretty smart."

"It sure is. But with all that knowledge of the brain, would that Mormon scientist who had never tasted espresso know what espresso tastes like?"

Sheridan leans back in his chair and squints as if deep in thought. After a long pause he answers, "To be honest, I'm not sure."

I nod in acknowledgment. "That's a fair response. At the very least it's reasonable to conclude that the scientist would not know the taste of coffee even after knowing all the brain states that accompany the drinking of coffee."

"Maybe. I said I'm not sure."

"Right, 'maybe.' But that 'maybe' is significant. Saying 'maybe' means that maybe somebody can know everything about a person's brain and still not know what's going on in their mind. And that suggests that the mind is something more than the functioning of the brain."

"How so?"

"Think of C. S. Lewis's book *The Lion, the Witch and the Wardrobe*. In the book young Lucy discovers a portal into a wintry land—a portal inside a large manor house. When she describes this land to her siblings—including a dark forest, a lamp post and a faun—they don't believe her. After all, they've explored every inch of the house and know there's no place for such a world. They're right. You can't fit Narnia into the floor plan of the house. But Lucy's right, too, because Narnia exists beyond the country house. The relationship between the brain and consciousness is something like the relationship between the house and Narnia. When we look for consciousness within the brain, we can't find it—consciousness seems to be a reality that transcends that three-pound lump of grey matter altogether."

Sheridan laughs. "The soul is like Narnia? I knew it! I bet deep down you really do believe in pixies and leprechauns."

"Geez, you may need to talk to someone about your obsession with pixies, Sheridan. But I think you're missing the point of my illustration. Let me try a famous philosophical thought experiment instead. It was first developed by eighteenth-century philosopher Leibniz. He suggested that we imagine a brain the size of a vast factory into which human beings could enter. If we walked into this giant brain, then everywhere we would see neurons firing—"

"Wait a minute," Sheridan interrupts. "Leibniz knew about neurons?"

"Not exactly. I'm updating the thought experiment a little." Sheridan looks skeptical. "Artistic license, Sheridan. It doesn't change the thought experiment. Leibniz points out that everywhere we'd see neurons firing but nowhere would we see conscious experience. Let's say that we shrink down to the size of a neuron and enter the brain of a person who is eating root-beer-flavored ice cream. We'd see the neurons crackling in the brain, but we'd never see or otherwise encounter the taste of root-beer ice cream. Leibniz used that type of scenario to argue that our mind cannot simply be our brain because we can know all about the brain and still not have access to the mind—like our espresso-studying neurologist."

Sheridan nods. "I follow the argument, but I'm not convinced that the problem doesn't just arise from our present ignorance. Right now we can't see yet how consciousness is the same thing as the firing of neurons, but I bet we will."

"Okay, remember when I mentioned the square circle? Would you agree that we can know a circle cannot be square? Or would you say only that you can't see how a circle could be square?"

"I'd agree with that. We can see that a circle cannot be square."

"I'm arguing something similar about consciousness. Conceptually speaking, we can see that a particular pattern of neurons firing cannot be the same thing as the experience of drinking espresso or eating ice cream. They're categorically different in nature."

Sheridan looks skeptical. "That certainly isn't as obvious as the square circle. What does all this have to do with a soul?"

"As I said, in the same way that Narnia's wintry wood transcends the architecture of the country house, so conscious life transcends the architecture of the brain."

"And how is this all supposed to relate to God?"

"First, this argument throws into question your claim that souls don't exist. On the contrary, I'd argue based on the evidence that conscious life is rooted in the soul. And once you recognize the evidence that immaterial souls may exist, the existence of an immaterial deity becomes that much more plausible. So your assumption that you can just take God out of the picture and leave everything else unchanged is simplistic. And one more thing—if it's plausible to view the mind as a non-physical substance that interacts with the brain, then it increases the plausibility of the idea that there could be another non-physical substance that interacts with the universe. Any guesses at what that non-physical substance might be called, Sheridan?" I ask with a smile.

Sheridan rolls his eyes.

14

The Pastry I Freely Choose

*** * ***

Maybe consciousness isn't the exact same thing as neurons firing," Sheridan concedes, "but it still could be a byproduct of neurons firing, couldn't it? Maybe our mind is produced by the brain much the same way that smoke is produced by a fire."

"That's an interesting suggestion, Sheridan. In fact it sounds a lot like epiphenomenalism, the view that the mind arises out of the functioning of the brain."

"Yeah, that's right," Sheridan nods in agreement. "That's what I'm saying."

"Unfortunately, epiphenomenalism runs into a serious problem with free will." At this point I pause and look around to find a good illustration. "You see the older gentleman by the pastry case?" I gesture toward a disheveled man wearing a tweed jacket and derby cap who's staring at the fresh-baked choices.

Sheridan nods. "Oh sure, that's Dr. Ferry. He's a pretty weird duck. I had him last year in biology."

"Which pastry do you think he'll choose?" I ask. As we look on, Dr. Ferry's intense gaze sweeps back and forth across the display.

"Definitely the rhubarb muffins," Sheridan says, nodding confidently. "Heated in the toaster oven with a pat of freshly churned butter. Can't be beat."

"I vote for the cinnamon buns," I reply.

At that moment Dr. Ferry taps the glass and says something inaudible to us. Immediately one of the baristas reaches in with a pair of tongs to retrieve one of the Beatnik Bean's famously sticky cinnamon buns. "Okay, maybe I lost that one," Sheridan concedes, "but I didn't hear you actually place a bet."

"That's because I knew he'd go for the cinnamon bun," I quip, "and I didn't want to steal your money. But the interesting thing is that we can explain that event with respect to Dr. Ferry's brain or his mind. Let's start with the physiological, brain-based explanation. According to this account, a certain pattern of photons hit Dr. Ferry's eyes. That sensory stimulation in turn caused a pattern of neurons to fire in his brain. Next, another pattern of neurons fired, causing muscles in his arm to contract and his finger to tap the glass. So we go from photons to neurons to muscles to finger-tapping. That's the physiological, brain-based account of how Dr. Ferry ends up with a cinnamon bun on his plate."

"Sounds good."

"Unfortunately, this explanation leaves out the crucial role of Dr. Ferry's mind. There's more than just neurons involved in the explanation of how a cinnamon bun ended up on his plate."

"And that is?"

"His mental desire for the cinnamon bun and his intention to order it to meet that desire. In fact, if you want the most important explanation for why his finger tapped on the glass you can't look simply to deaf, dumb and blind neurons. You've got to look to Dr. Ferry's mental intention to order a cinnamon bun because he wanted one."

"Okay . . . ?" Sheridan looks lost.

"Sheridan, you suggested that mental events—sensations, desires, intentions and the like—are mere byproducts of the firing of neurons like smoke rising from fire. If that's the case then they have no role to play in the story of Dr. Ferry's ordering a cinnamon bun. All of Dr. Ferry's actions are determined and thus explained by the firing of neurons in his brain while his mind does nothing. But this doesn't seem to match reality at all, does it? Surely Dr. Ferry's intention to order a cinnamon bun is causally basic in the story of how one ends up on his plate. It's because he wanted a cinnamon bun that a particular pattern of neurons fired, causing his finger to tap the glass. And it's because he wanted to express this intention that more neurons fired, thereby causing him to vocalize the desire to have one to the barista.

"So that's two reasons to support the existence of a mind or soul in addition to the brain. First, conscious experience is something more than the activity of the brain. And second, our minds interact in the physical world. This means that we have at least one example of a non-physical substance—a mind or soul—that interacts with the physical world. And if souls can exist and interact with the world, then why not think that God could be another non-physical substance that interacts with the world?"

I grin. "Who would have thought that you could learn so much from a quirky old professor buying a cinnamon bun?"

"Dude!" Sheridan hisses as he gestures over my shoulder. I turn around slowly and to my horror see Dr. Ferry sitting at the table behind us and staring right at me.

15

Naturalism, Scientism and the Screwdriver That Could Fix Almost Anything

* * *

This is awkward. As Dr. Ferry butters his cinnamon bun, he continues to look at me suspiciously. Much to my relief, Sheridan breaks the uncomfortable tension. "Listen," he says as he stands, "how about we take a commercial break here? I gotta take a whiz."

"You bet." I nod, relieved for a way out of the awkward moment. "It's hard to unpack the mysteries of the universe on a full bladder."

As Sheridan walks away, I look over to you. I can tell what you're thinking: isn't it a bit crass to include a bathroom break in a book like this? After all, Socrates never takes a bathroom break in Plato's dialogues. Why don't I treat my characters like bladderless talking heads?

"Verisimilitude," I whisper to you. "I'm trying to make this as lifelike as possible. In fact, Reader, in order to maximize realism I think I'll take a quick bathroom break myself. I don't want to play the omniscient narrator here, you know? I've got to be in the story to be credible." With that I stand up and walk over to the cash register to grab the remaining washroom key.

When I return a few minutes later, you and Sheridan are sitting quietly and Sheridan has a fresh steaming cappuccino sitting on the coffee table. "Reader was just trying to guess what's going on in my soul as I drink this cappuccino," Sheridan jokes.

I roll my eyes. "Always the showman. So where were we?"

"You were arguing that consciousness and free will exist and that's good news for the God hypothesis somehow. I'm not so sure. I still think we should stick with what we can show through science."

"Hey," I smile, "now we're getting into something more substantial than you simply being without belief in God. Does that claim about science mean that you're a naturalist?"

"What do you mean by 'naturalist'? Are you asking whether I like granola and organic foods, or what?"

I chuckle. "Not quite. If I'm following you, then your skepticism about angels and souls, consciousness and free will, all trace back to your commitment to science, right?"

"I'd say so. I don't see any need to say there's a God or angels or souls or leprechauns or pixies."

"To put it another way, you could say that there is no supernature."

"Supernature?"

"Right—no dimension to existence that transcends the natural world of matter and force that's studied by science. That's your view, right?"

"Yes," Sheridan answers cautiously, as if looking for a trap. "I'd say that there is no supernature . . . just like you think there are no leprechauns."

"Geez, man, first pixies and now a leprechaun obsession? Is it because you're Irish?" Sheridan makes a face as I continue. "I want to bring this back to the question of epistemic justification. What justifies your belief that there is no supernature and that everything is explicable in terms of science? I've provided arguments from consciousness and free will that suggest there is more to the world than that. So what is your positive argument for naturalism?"

"Wait up," Sheridan replies. "I'm not claiming to have an answer for everything. I don't know how consciousness or free will works, but that doesn't mean I'm going to conclude right away that 'God did it'! That's just the 'god of the gaps' fallacy. What I am saying is that the scientist has proven to be the go-to person to understand the world. Scientists keep explaining more and more of the stuff that we used to explain with religion, like weather events and diseases. So why wouldn't you think that science could eventually explain everything?"

"Because that doesn't follow! Look, let me take a step back to summarize what I hear you saying. First, you believe that science can explain everything. That's a form of 'scientism.' But there's more, because you're not only making a claim about science's ability to explain whatever exists. You're also claiming that no supernature exists. You recognize that something non-physical like consciousness might exist, but you insist that if it does then it must ultimately be dependent upon the physical brain. Is that about right?" Sheridan nods. "So it sounds like you believe that the only things that exist are matter and energy and that which supervenes upon matter and energy. Do you agree?"

"Maybe. I'll let you know when you tell me what you mean by 'supervene.'"

"Supervenience refers to a type of dependence relationship. If A supervenes on B, then A is constituted by B and depends on B for its existence, but it is not reducible to B. It is something altogether different. Perhaps the easiest way to explain the concept of super-venience is by way of an example. Neither hydrogen atoms nor oxygen atoms have the property of wetness. But combine them to form a water molecule and the property of wetness comes to exist as a result of the combined atoms. In other words, it supervenes upon them. In the same way I heard you saying that conscious events may not be the exact same thing as brain events, but they still supervene on the firing of neurons."

"Sure, that makes sense, don't you think? Wetness just arises out of the combination of atoms and consciousness arises out of the combination of neurons." Sheridan smirks. "Or do you believe that water is divinely wet?"

"I certainly agree that wetness supervenes on the combination of hydrogen and oxygen atoms—that's why I gave the example! But the person who accepts this definition of naturalism believes that everything that is not material supervenes on the material. In this view, the ultimate ground-level explanation for everything is matter in motion. Thus the naturalist is one who says that everything that exists is either matter/energy or supervenes upon matter/energy."

"That's a brain squeezer, so let me get this straight. By accepting naturalism one denies that anything exists that doesn't ultimately derive its existence from matter/energy. And that excludes souls, angels and God."

"That's right."

"I guess I would sign on to that definition. I accept scientism, at least as a provisional thesis, and I don't think there is any super-nature: no gods, angels or souls. And if there is a conscious mind beyond the firing of neurons then it supervenes on the brain."

"Good. So that brings me to my question: Why do you think that scientism and naturalism are true? Take naturalism. Why do you think that the only things that exist are matter, energy and that which supervenes upon matter and energy?"

"That's easy. The explanation is simpler than the alternatives."

I raise my hand in an emphatic stop motion. "Wait a minute! What makes it simpler?"

Sheridan crosses his arms. "It posits fewer entities to explain the data."

"If simplicity is the only thing you're concerned with in expla-nations, then you can justify a pretty extreme view of the world in the name of simplicity—remember idealism and solipsism? Or you could give up on the idea of a soul . . . but then you'd have to surrender the commonsense assumption that we have free will. So if our only consideration is to minimize explanatory posits, we could all become solipsists. But that can't be right. Don't we need a place for common sense as well?"

"I see what you're trying to do and I ain't sliding down that slippery slope, pal. I'm not saying that common sense isn't of any value. But neither can you expect me to buy into your medieval brand of common sense."

"What exactly are you calling 'medieval'?"

"We don't need pixies to explain the world anymore and we don't need God. There's simply no evidence for the supernatural."

"That's a pretty bald claim. Most people would disagree with you—and that includes people in every society in the world. They see no incompatibility between the existence of God and the modern technological world. The bottom line is that you still haven't provided any reason to believe that scientism and naturalism are true."

"What do you think science won't be able to explain?"

"Ethics, aesthetics, free will, consciousness, all sorts of things. Science is obviously successful in its sphere, but it doesn't follow that it can explain everything."

"Wait a second," Sheridan says. "If you don't have to provide evidence for the non-existence of leprechauns, why do I have to provide evidence for the non-existence of angels and souls or your whole supernature?"

"I may not initially have any burden to disprove the existence of leprechauns, but that changes when I meet people who earnestly believe in them. Let's say that I discover that my next-door neighbor Quinn O'Malley and his clan are convinced that leprechauns exist. If I want to disabuse Quinn of this belief, then I do have a burden to demonstrate that leprechauns do not exist. Leprechaun believers are few and far between, but most people on the earth, not to mention nearly everyone in history, believe in the existence of God. If you want to have anything to say to them you have a burden of proof to meet.

"And," I say, trying to finish my point, "your burden of proof is not only to argue against Christianity and theism. It's also to argue for scientism and naturalism. And those theses are a lot more contentious than the personal agnosticism I first heard you describe. You're not just saying that you're without belief in God. Now you've made positive claims about the nature of the world and science that must be defended."

"I can see why you'd want to claim that I need to do that, but positively showing that naturalism is true seems impossible."

"That's a strange objection! Would it make sense if I shirked the demand to provide evidence for my Christian beliefs by saying that I simply can't provide any so I'm not obliged to? If I can't defend my beliefs, then maybe I shouldn't hold them. Doesn't the same thing go for you? If you can't defend your beliefs, then maybe you shouldn't hold them. In fact, I find that protest doubly ironic since you already suggested a way that you could argue for the truth of naturalism."

"Did I?" Sheridan asks with surprise.

"Yeah, you said that naturalism is a simpler explanation. Now I took issue with that claim by saying that if simplicity is your only consideration then you should go further and be an idealist or even a solipsist. But even if I don't accept your simplicity argument, it illustrates that in principle naturalism can be defended by argument."

Sheridan leans back in his chair and furrows his eyebrows, deep in thought. "Well, I'm going to stick with scientism. Science explains more and more every year, so why not think it can go all the way eventually? I don't see any reason that science won't explain ethics and art someday." He points at my empty coffee cup. "As I have noted, espresso is the product of science, not religion.

And caffeine gets more people out of bed in the morning than God does, I guarantee."

I must say I find myself underwhelmed by this piece of reasoning. Not that I want to undersell the power of caffeine, but a substitute for deity? Please. "Sheridan," I say, "it's like you're taking a useful tool and then erroneously applying it to every task. That's a big mistake. Just consider the case of Don the construction worker."

"Don the construction worker?" Sheridan rolls his eyes. "This sounds like a children's story."

"The moral is simple enough for a children's story. One day Don bought a new screwdriver with a shiny red handle and a number of removable bits. With great aplomb Don began using his new screwdriver for slotted screws of all different sizes. But then one day he discovered that it had another bit that fit Phillips screws, and soon he was off again working on every Phillips screw in sight. Shortly thereafter he encountered a strange screw with a square hole. For awhile he tried jamming in various slotted and Phillips bits, but nothing worked. Then, just when Don was about to throw in the towel, he discovered a square bit! Yes, his screwdriver could even handle that strange Canadian import, the Robertson screw."

Sheridan gives me an impatient look. "Can you move this along please? This isn't story hour at the library."

"Tut tut. Patience. As I was saying, Don was positively enamored with his screwdriver and its seemingly limitless use on the construction site. If you needed to screw anything up, Don was the man to do it." Sheridan actually cracks a smile, albeit a withering one, at my attempt at a pun.

"One day Don's fellow workers were shocked to see him attempting to hammer in a nail with the handle of his screwdriver. Tentatively they informed him that his screwdriver was made for screws, and that the driving of nails requires a hammer, not a screwdriver—even one as fine as Don's. But, alas, Don would not listen. So impressed was he with the power of his tool to put every screw in its place that he became convinced it must be good for nails, too. Later in the day Don was seen trying to cut a plank of wood with the screwdriver. As the other workers packed up for the night, Don could be spotted attempting to sand a banister with his screwdriver. Needless to say, all he succeeded in doing was gouging the wood. Poor Don never learned the important lesson that even the best tools have their limits."

"Aesop it ain't," Sheridan says.

"Granted, I didn't include any talking animals to hold your attention," I reply, "but don't miss the point. It seems that you're bedazzled with the marvelous achievements of that fine tool we call science in much the same way that Don was smitten by his screwdriver. There is no question that science is a marvelously useful tool. The problem arises when some people think they can apply science to every task, including art, literature, ethics and religion. That's when things get a little wacky. It reminds me of a scene in the film *Dead Poets Society* where John Keating—"

"Played by Robin Williams. That movie's one of my favorites."

"Right, so remember the scene where he instructs his students to rip out the introductory article to their literature textbook, which was written by this stuffed shirt named 'J. Evans Pritchard'? Keating is incensed that Pritchard has advised the reader to assess poetry 'scientifically' by composing a scale with two axes and numeric values so that poems can be charted and rated 'objectively.' Keating's response is classic. 'Excrement!' he says. 'That's what I think of Mr. J. Evans Pritchard! We're not laying pipe. We're talking about poetry!' And he's exactly right. It's the scientific mindset run amok that thinks science can provide an exhaustive analysis of poetry, or ethics, art or religion."

"So you think poor Screwdriver Don is full of excrement?"

"I wouldn't put it that way, but Keating would. Let's just say that Don is seriously misguided. A screwdriver is a great tool, but it can't do everything. And one can think that science is wonderful for all sorts of tasks, but one need not think that it can thereby explain everything. If you insist on trying to explain everything with science, you'll do little more than bend a lot of nails."

"Another Procrustean bed?"

"Exactly. Instead of trying to bang nails with the screwdriver, why not take another look in the toolbox and see what else you've got to work with? Believe me, the screwdriver won't mind."

16

God as a Simple Answer

★ ★ ★

Sheridan leans back in his chair and runs his hand through his hair. "I must admit," he says, "you're pretty good at attacking the views of others. First you tried to argue that I'm really an agnostic, and then you tried to nail me for holding to versions of scientism and naturalism that you apparently don't like."

"Hey, wait a minute. You said that science can explain everything and that everything is either reducible to or dependent on matter and force. I didn't put words in your mouth."

"Yeah, yeah, yeah." Sheridan waves his hand dismissively. "But," he adds with emphasis, "I still haven't heard a single thing to convince me that your belief in the Christian God is any more reasonable than belief in Zeus."

"Okay, so you want to know what justifies a Christian in choosing one particular definition of God over another?"

"Of course! I get that you're claiming God is experienced in some kind of basic or immediate way. Of course children think they experience pixies and sprites in a basic way, too. But I don't experience God at all, so if the big kahuna is going to get any consideration from me, it's going to be as a hypothesis to explain what

I do experience. Unfortunately, on that score the God hypothesis is completely useless.

"Sheridan, you remember how I pointed out that judgments of plausibility are made relative to a background set of beliefs? One person's astonishing hypothesis is another person's common sense. I also noted that simplicity is a relative value since we are typically willing to accept a more complex view of the world if doing so enables us to maintain more of our commonsense assumptions."

"Yeah, so?"

"So, many people have argued that positing God enables us to maintain much more of our common sense than we would be able to do otherwise. We already talked about consciousness and free will. God also provides a powerful explanation for other dimensions of our experience, including the objective nature of morality and meaning."

"What do you mean 'objective'?"

"I mean a fact that is true whether or not any human being believes it."

"Okay, but what keeps your God hypothesis from simply being various claims cherry-picked out of the air, a fabricated imaginary creature to explain everything? It's like painting the target around the arrow after the fact. It's completely arbitrary. Why stop at one God?"

"What are you talking about?"

"Think about it. If Billy is going to insist that we need to posit pixies that move the pine trees every time it gets windy, why doesn't he also attribute the waves in the sea to sprites working overtime? If he invokes one weird explanation, then he has no reason not to invoke others. Once he starts down this road, he should just keep expanding his catalogue of esoteric little beasties until he's got a bizarre explanation for the movement of every pebble."

"What relevance does that have to God?" I ask.

Sheridan waves his finger in my face for emphasis. "You've got the same dilemma, buddy. Either you should admit that Zeus might also exist, along with all the other neglected and forgotten gods of history, or you should admit that there's no reason to accept any gods. Right now you're trying to justify your belief in your trinity Yahweh God as the one exception that actually exists. That makes about as much sense as insisting that Dopey Dwarf is real but that all the other dwarves in Snow White's merry crew are fictional."

"Dopey Dwarf?" I exclaim. "That's rhetorically effective, I'll give you that. But it's also a misleading comparison. Saying that only Dopey exists would be arbitrary because it would amount to selecting one character out of a narrative as historical while rejecting the rest of the narrative. I'm not doing that. I'm saying that one complete narrative is true and others are false. That's no more arbitrary than a scientist accepting one theory and rejecting another."

"Okay, Randal, then how about this for an analogy? It's like you accept that all of Aesop's fables are fiction except for the Tortoise and the Hare. You insist that that story really happened." Sheridan suddenly starts to laugh. "Sorry, dude, that's funny. But it's true. You reject all the other fairy tales but you insist that your sky God really did come to earth and rose back up into the clouds. That's not just arbitrary. It's crazy."

"There is good evidence for the resurrection of Jesus, unlike other ancient miracle reports," I reply. "If there was evidence that the hare really raced the tortoise, I'd consider it, too. I've got an open mind."

"Randal, you got two billion people in your religion desperately trying to find some reason to believe in Jesus, looking for any shred of evidence. Is it any surprise that they managed to scrounge up more scraps of evidence than other ancient miracle reports? If two billion people believed that Elvis was alive, no doubt they could also come up with a lot of 'evidence.'"

"Sheridan, it doesn't matter how many people want something to be true. Either the historical evidence is there or it isn't, and in this case it is. Rather than talk vaguely about 'shreds of evidence' I think you should read up in New Testament scholarship."

"Nice self-serving suggestion, Randy. 'Read up in the Bible teachers.' Sorry, I actually have a life."

"Listen, I'd like to go back to the general question of God as an explanation."

"Good idea. If you can show that God is a sensible hypothesis for anything, then I'm listening, bro."

"Okay," I say, "I'll concede that without further explanation it might be arbitrary to invoke a specific description of God, be it Yahweh or Zeus. But even if these specific token descriptions are arbitrary without further explanation, it doesn't follow that God as a type of explanation is."

"Uh—what?"

"Here's an illustration. I leave my keys on the kitchen table. When I come back later, they're on the floor. Logically speaking, there's an infinite number of ways my keys could have ended up there, but ultimately there are only two basic types of explanation: a non-intelligent cause and an intelligent cause. That is, either some undirected process like a seismic tremor knocked my keys on the floor, or a person put them on the floor."

"So to say it is intelligent is to say it is human?"

"Not necessarily. There are conceivably other intelligences that could have moved the keys, like a dog, or even a poltergeist, for instance."

Immediately Sheridan brightens. "I like the poltergeist option!" he says with palpable enthusiasm. "That reminds me of the horror film *Paranormal Activity*. There's a scene where Katie comes down to the kitchen in the morning and finds her keys on the floor even though she left them on the counter the night before."

"Right, so whenever an event like that occurs we can ask if a 'what' caused the event—a non-intelligent cause—or if it was a 'who'—an intelligent cause."

"That's how it is for Katie. She hopes the explanation is something impersonal, but unfortunately for her it's a rather angry demon."

"Too bad for Katie," I say sympathetically. "That must stink, having demons moving your keys. So distilled down to its essence, seeking an explanation for events in the world is first of all seeking to answer whether there is an agent involved."

"Sure, but how do you get from an agent moving your keys to God?"

17

A Giant Mickey Mouse Balloon and the Keebler Elves

* * *

Good question, Sheridan. Let's consider one point where the 'God explanation' enters the picture. Consider one of the most basic questions there is: 'Why is there something rather than nothing?' That's a question that can be answered with the same two options we use when explaining the movement of Katie's keys. Is the origin of the universe best explained by a personal agent cause or an impersonal event cause? At the very least, asking whether the universe has a personal cause is not hopelessly arbitrary. Rather, it's a simple and very reasonable question. Consequently, God is a very reasonable question to be asking."

"Hold on! 'Consequently God is reasonable'? I think I missed something. Even if it's reasonable in principle to ask whether the universe had a personal cause, that doesn't mean it's reasonable to conclude that it does. Like I said, maybe the universe just exists, full stop. That's it."

"It just exists for no reason at all? Full stop? Okay, let's think about this a bit. Imagine that you're walking in the woods when you come across a helium-filled Mickey Mouse balloon floating a few feet above the forest floor. Wouldn't you wonder how that balloon got there?" Sheridan shrugs. "Surely you would agree that there must be a reason why that balloon exists. If somebody said, 'No, the balloon just exists, full stop!' you'd think they were acting crazy. Now imagine now that our Mickey Mouse balloon is inflated to the size of the universe. Does the size of the balloon suddenly make the question 'Why is there a Mickey Mouse balloon rather than nothing?' uninteresting? Does it suddenly make the answer 'The balloon just exists, full stop!' plausible?"

Sheridan rolls his eyes. "The universe isn't a Mickey Mouse balloon."

"But why is that relevant? Whether we're talking about the balloon or the universe, we have a contingent material object that requires a cause for its existence."

"For the balloon, sure, but I just don't think that's true for the universe. That's the fallacy of composition. You're erroneously inferring something of the whole just because it applies to the parts. You can't do that. Even if every object in the universe requires a cause for its existence, that doesn't mean the universe itself does. It is simpler to just say the universe exists."

"Sheridan, for there to be a fallacy here you need to be able to show how a universe constituted of contingent entities is itself necessarily existent. Unless you have some reason to believe that the whole doesn't require a cause for its existence, it's legitimate to move from the contingency of the parts to the contingency of the whole. So what reason do you have, apart from your desire to avoid the existence of God?"

"So who caused God? You've got an infinite regress, pal. If everything needs an explanation, then God does too. If God doesn't need an explanation, then neither does the universe."

"I didn't say everything needs an explanation. I said contingent things need explanations. The universe is a contingent entity. The reason we know this is because there's nothing in the concept of a 'material universe' that requires its existence, and we can readily conceive a state of affairs in which the universe never came to exist. So it is meaningful to seek an explanation for its existence. And to avoid that infinite regress you mentioned, we have to invoke a necessary cause, something which is not itself contingent."

"So why do you get to say the cause is God? Isn't that, like, raising all kinds of questions?"

"Let's amend our balloon illustration to take note of big bang cosmology. Imagine that fourteen billion years ago there was nothing, and then suddenly a Mickey Mouse balloon sprang into existence out of nothing and that balloon has been inflating ever since. Doesn't that make you even more inclined to think that there must be some reason for the beginning of its existence?"

"I'm not buying it. Even if the universe does have a reason for its existence, why does God automatically get the credit? Maybe some super-advanced alien civilization created the universe."

I look skeptical. "What are you talking about?"

"A physicist named Michio Kaku argues that an alien civilization could possibly have developed a technology so advanced that it could create universes. Kaku's speculations allow us to consider that super-advanced aliens from another universe may have created our universe. You can't just assume that the cause is God."

"Wait a minute!" I say. "So God is 'crazy' but super-intelligent universe-creating aliens are fine? Even if that were the case, you could still ask what reason there is that the aliens' universe exists."

"Maybe it was created by aliens from another universe," Sheridan says with a wicked grin.

"And maybe it was created by leprechauns! You have officially lost the right to call any of my beliefs crazy."

Sheridan laughs. "I don't know why everything has to have an explanation. I think the universe just exists. But even if you think the universe has a personal cause, there's still a huge leap from that type of explanation to a particular religious explanation like your trinity Yahweh. How is your God a simple explanation of anything?"

"That's a good question," I admit. "For one thing, you should keep in mind that 'personal agent cause of the universe' is consistent with Christian theism, but it doesn't tell the whole story. I'm not claiming that being a Christian is as simple as believing there's a personal cause of the universe. But opting to believe that there is a personal agent cause behind the universe raises the question of how that cause should be described. Once we're in a place to recognize such a being, we can consider what description of this personal agent cause might be appropriate or what we can know of it."

"So how are you going to get to trinity Yahweh instead of Zeus? How can you justify your particular description of this personal agent cause?"

"Okay, once we believe that an agent caused an event like the universe's origin, we can then consider which agent caused the event. It doesn't need to be divine, but it's very plausible to consider it divine."

"Maybe, but there's no need to go as far as the Christian God, unless you can find 'Jesus was here' written into our DNA or something like that. Now that would be great evidence!"

"Well, let's consider this character Katie again. How does she conclude that a demon moved her keys?"

"I guess she eliminated non-intelligent options because there was no earthquake or other plausible natural explanation. As for personal causes, her boyfriend Micah didn't move the keys, she doesn't have any pets, and nobody else was in the house."

"So what led her to conclude that it was a demon?"

"She already had reason to believe that a demon was tormenting her, so it just made sense to assume that the demon moved the keys."

"Interesting. That's helpful. You see, whenever we try to explain an event there are all sorts of possible non-intelligent and intelligent causes we could invoke—an infinite number, in fact. But, like Katie, we exclude all but a few from consideration, and we do so based on our experience and background beliefs. To an extent, this may seem arbitrary—a person can always object that we haven't exhausted every possible alternative explanation—but the fact is that we all have to start somewhere. That's true when we're trying to explain why a set of keys were moved, and it's also true when scientists formulate hypotheses and construct theories. When it comes to natural events there are also an infinite number of possible non-intelligent and intelligent causes, but the scientist excludes the vast majority out of the gate and only considers a few as live candidates. And this is the way it must be or a scientist could never formulate a single specific hypothesis or test a single specific theory."

"Let me guess: you're going to say the same thing about God?"

"Why not? What's true in everyday experience and scientific inquiry is also true when we move into grand metaphysical questions like 'Why is there something rather than nothing?' If I believe there are good grounds for concluding that a personal agent caused the universe, I can then make the reasonable leap of describing this being as the Christian God, at least provisionally. And I can do this without giving Zeus or any other god a second thought, just like Katie concludes a demon moved her keys without considering that a ninja or E.T. broke into her house and surreptitiously moved her keys. All of us exclude almost the entire number of possible explanations of an event at the outset, whether we're seeking to explain moved keys or the origin of the universe. So I'm not asking for a special exception when I take the personal cause to be Yahweh."

"But that's arbitrary, Randal. If you were an ancient Greek, then Zeus—or Cronus or whoever created things; my myth knowledge is rusty—would definitely be a live option. It's not that most Americans today have a well-thought-out argument against Zeus's existence. The poor deity just doesn't come on the radar screen to begin with."

"Sure, I agree. But remember, for scientists throughout history certain theoretical possibilities have been live options in hypothesis and theory formation, and others have not. So whether you're a scientist, a devout religious person or anything else, the same fact remains. We all have to exclude most possibilities when we're surveying potential non-intelligent and intelligent causes. Asking why we choose Yahweh over Zeus is simply a particular example of a very common question: 'Why this causal explanation rather than another?' And that question is faced by everybody all the time, whether we're looking for our keys or the origin of the universe."

"So that's your argument, huh? Since we all exclude most explanatory options, it's okay for the Christian to assume Yahweh is God? Man, you're like a busker who only knows how to play one song: *tu quoque* over and over."

"I keep coming back to the *tu quoque* because you consistently attempt to pose a problem or dilemma for Christians that's part of a general problem or dilemma everybody faces. Once again you're trying to get my Trans-Am towed while ignoring the implications that has for your big old Winnebago."

Sheridan looks unsatisfied. "There's something tricky about that kind of argument," he says. "I can sniff out a debater's trick from a mile away."

I don't know if Sheridan is trying to irk me, but this certainly does. "Debater's trick?" I snort. "Accusing the other guy of a debater's trick because you can't answer his argument—now that's a real debater's trick."

"Hold on," Sheridan interjects. "How do you know the Keebler Elves didn't move Katie's keys? After all, the keys were left in the kitchen right near the cookies."

I give Sheridan a long look. His invocation of the Keebler Elves is intended as a slur against theism, as if one "absurd" explanation deserved another. Fine, I'll play along. "The Keebler Elves were created by a marketing agency for the Keebler company to sell their cookies. So in that case I have a plausible natural explanation of their origin—and with it I have a defeater to anyone who actually believes the little creatures move anything except boxes of product."

18

From Personal Cause to Most Perfect Being

* * *

Sheridan, I'm certainly not claiming that the statement 'personal cause of the universe' is a religiously satisfactory definition of God. But even if that description doesn't say all a Christian wants to say about God, it certainly says something important. Christians believe that God is the creator of all things and thus that the question 'Why is there something rather than nothing?' has a personal answer: God."

"But can you come up with a reason for believing in Yahweh that's more substantial than the lame claim that it happens to be a 'live option' for you?"

"Before getting to Yahweh, let's see if we can add more specificity to the general concept of God. The medieval theologian Anselm defined God as 'that being than which none greater can be conceived.' In other words, God is the greatest conceivable or most perfect being. It is not possible to conceive a greater being."

"That's still a pretty abstract philosophical description for a Christian, isn't it?"

"Perhaps. You could also argue that it's actually pretty trivial. I mean, if God exists, he simply must be the most perfect being. But as long as we're positing God, it's legitimate to define God as the most perfect being there could be."

"Fine, but then where do you go with that definition?"

"Well, saying that provides a helpful way to eliminate those descriptions that fail to meet the demands of the definition. Take the Mormon concept of God as an example. Mormons believe that the God of the Bible was once a man who evolved over time and became divine. In fact, they believe that Yahweh is just one of infinitely many creatures who have evolved to have divine powers over time and that this same destiny awaits us as well if we work hard enough at it."

"Seriously? I thought Mormons were Christians."

"Kudos to the Latter-day Saints marketing arm, then. From the historical Christian point of view, if we start with the definition of 'greatest possible being' or 'that being than which none greater can be conceived,' then we find that the Mormon concept of God is excluded out of the gate. The difference between me and that deity is like the difference between a junior athlete and an Olympian: that is, one of degree rather than kind. But surely if God is the most perfect being, then he differs from us in kind, not merely degree. So if I accept Anselm's definition, then I won't treat the Mormon concept as a 'live option.'"

"Don't get me wrong, Randal. I think Mormonism is whacked, too. But your analysis still strikes me as pretty self-serving."

"How so?"

"You exclude the Mormon concept because it's beneath your definition. No surprise there. But then you find it sensible to say that God would submit to torture and death at the hands of human beings. Why don't you ask a Muslim what they think of the idea that God became a baby with dirty diapers and grew up to be tortured to death!"

"That's a fair point," I admit. "It's true that we all differ to some degree in our notion of perfection. So I admit that a Muslim would not fully agree with my understanding of perfection. But at the same time, you can't say God is whatever you like. I think the Anselmic concept is so basic that every description of God has to be held up to it. If a particular concept of God appears to result in a deity that's less than perfect, then we need to revise either our understanding of God or our understanding of perfection. But we can't say God is less than perfect."

"Okay, so you believe your sky God is perfect, despite all the evidence to the contrary. But why even think that your God exists? Just because you come up with a description of God doesn't mean that your God is real. You can't just define God into existence. Look, I've got the idea of the most perfect summer vacation home in my head: a mansion on a white-sand tropical beach with gardens like Versailles, a giant hot tub and a limitless supply of beer in the fridge. I'd go to the mat arguing that I cannot conceive of a greater vacation home than this, but so what? The fact that I can define a perfect vacation home doesn't mean it exists. In fact, I'm pretty sure it doesn't exist. So even if you use this perfection idea to exclude certain definitions of God as inadequate, why think that this most perfect being exists to begin with?"

"You're exactly right, Sheridan—it's crucial to ask whether the greatest conceivable being exists. Remember, earlier I did say that if God existed he would be the most perfect being. So let's come at that question in a roundabout way by asking if it's possible that the greatest conceivable being exists. Is it?"

Sheridan answers cautiously: "Possible? I'm not sure. Maybe."

"Okay, let's ask about some other things and come back to the greatest conceivable being. Is it possible that your vacation home exists? In other words, even if it doesn't in fact exist, could it have existed?"

"Yeah, sure, of course."

"And how about a square circle? Is it possible that such a shape exists?"

Sheridan looks at me like I'm crazy. "No, of course not," he retorts. "But what's the link between vacation homes and square circles?"

"Hang in there. Why is a square circle impossible?"

"Because it doesn't make sense, dude. It's contradictory."

"Right. So it is possible that the perfect vacation home exists, but it's not possible that a square circle exists. And when you make those judgments you're relying on the fact that if an entity is not contradictory then it might exist, but if it is contradictory then it can't exist."

"Yeah, sure. And hey, uh, feel free to come back to God anytime, Randal."

"I'm getting there. So if we think about the infinite number of ways that things could have happened, your vacation home exists in some of those ways, but not in others. But in none of the ways things could have happened is there a square circle. That's just impossible, contradictory, right?"

Sheridan pretends to start snoring, so I speed things along.

"So we have some things that might exist, like the perfect vacation home. If they do exist, then they exist contingently. That means they could have failed to exist. Other things could not exist, like a square circle. They necessarily do not exist. And thus a statement like 'There are no square circles' is necessarily true. Other things necessarily exist, like the numbers two and four."

"What do you mean that two and four necessarily exist?"

"Well, think about this: What would it take to destroy the number two? Could we build a big enough bomb to blow it up?"

"No, of course not," Sheridan laughs incredulously. "It's not that kind of thing."

"Right. Numbers don't exist in the same way that chairs, trees, mountains, planets and people do—but they do exist. Arithmetic, algebra and calculus are all knowledge discourses about an objective reality, not just concepts we invent. And mathematicians are the intrepid explorers in these stranger lands. Unlike chairs, trees, mountains, planets and people, which are all contingent, numbers exist necessarily. Consequently, no matter how things might have turned out, two and four would always exist. And that means that two plus two equals four would always be true."

Sheridan yawns. "That's great, but remember we were talking about God?"

"Well here we go: when it comes to God—the being than which none greater can be conceived—that being cannot exist contingently, like a beach house."

Sheridan sits up suspiciously. "Why not?"

"Because a being that must exist is, all things being equal, greater than one that only happens to exist but might not have existed."

"Who says?"

"I'm depending on an intuition to make that claim, but I think it is a strong intuition. Let's say that you have two beings that are indistinguishable except that one exists of necessity while the other exists only contingently. It seems to me that if we are going to say one is a higher being it is the one who exists necessarily. And if you grant that intuition, then if the greatest possible being exists, that being must exist. Those are our choices: If we accept the definition of God as the most perfect being, then it follows either that God must exist or it is not possible that God exists. To put it another way, if it's possible that God exists, then it's necessary that God exists."

Sheridan chuckles. "Sounds like you're trying to play 'double or nothing.' Either God exists necessarily or not at all."

"That's not too far off, although I wouldn't exactly characterize the discussion as a bet. It's really just a matter of definitions."

"So God can't exist contingently like the beach house? No problem. Then I'll say it's not possible God exists. That was easy!

Now where do I cash in my chips?"

"Not so fast. It's easy to demonstrate why a square circle isn't possible because there's a basic contradiction of properties in the concept. But what contradiction exists in the concept of a most perfect being? What is internally contradictory about the concept of God that would make it like a square circle?"

"There's another possibility. Maybe your definition of a 'most perfect being' is not even meaningful."

"What's not meaningful about the concept?"

"Well, in order to say there's a 'most perfect being,' everything that exists must be comparable to everything else: trees, planets, people, everything. Only then can you place God at the top of the scale. But that kind of absolute scale doesn't make any sense. You can't meaningfully say that a redwood tree is 'absolutely greater' than a tiger, can you? Those kinds of things are comparable within their classes but not beyond them. So the idea of a 'most perfect being' just doesn't make sense. It's like saying that the color red is more perfect than the sound of a waterfall."

"I agree that not everything is comparable in terms of absolute perfection to everything else. But it doesn't follow that everything is not comparable to God, does it? Even if we can't compare redwoods and tigers to each other in terms of perfection, it doesn't follow that we cannot compare them to God. And if God is the creator and sustainer of all things, then it seems very plausible to conclude that God is greater than all things."

"Look, even if there is a greatest being, even if there must be, why think that it has anything to do with your religion? There are thousands of deities in religion. So what makes you so sure that your God is the greatest?"

19

Why Zeus, at Least, Isn't God

* * *

That's another good question," I reply to Sheridan. "How about we take stock at this point? So far we're considering a simple description of God as the personal cause of the universe. The existence of the contingent universe is enough to show us that invoking God as an explanation is not arbitrary. Thus, being a theist does not oblige one to adopt an indefensibly complex, arbitrary view of the world. Further, reflection on the intuitively compelling definition of God as most perfect being shows that if it is possible that God exist, then God must exist."

Sheridan retorts, "Says you, maybe, but not me! I think it isn't possible. And even if those abstract philosophical descriptions work, they're still a world away from the descriptions of God I read in the Bible. The God of the philosophers may be squeaky clean, but the God of the Bible is covered with blood. So do you have some kind of proof to establish that trinity Yahweh is God rather than, say, Zeus? I mean, I get your basic point that people don't worship Zeus anymore so he isn't a live option for you, and Christianity is the religion thriving in your backyard so you begin defining the greatest being in that way. But is that really all you can say to exclude poor Zeus from the god contest? That seems so arbitrary. I want you to justify your dismissal of gone and forgotten gods with something more substantial than saying 'nobody worships those gods anymore.'"

"Fair enough. I think we could go about this a couple of ways. I could focus on disproving the existence of Zeus. But I could also try to argue that even if Zeus does exist, he is not that being than which none greater can be conceived."

"What? Did I hear you right? Are you leaving it open that Zeus might exist? Whoa, does the Bible school where you teach know about your pro-Zeus theology?"

"Just don't tell my tenure committee. Okay, hear me out. Let's start by considering what the Greeks taught about Zeus. According to Greek mythology, Zeus originated from copulation between Cronus and Rhea. Since he owes his existence to these other gods, Zeus cannot be the most perfect being anymore than the Mormon Yahweh can. Thus Zeus is not a legitimate object of worship."

"But he still might exist?"

"That's an interesting question." I nod toward a young woman with short hair sitting on a stool near the window reading a novel. "Let's say that you want to point out that person to me. How far off can you be in your description before you are no longer successfully referring to her?"

"I don't follow you."

"Well, let's say that she's drinking a decaf and you refer to her as 'the young woman drinking a caffeinated beverage.' Did you successfully refer to her?"

"Sure. That's not a big mistake."

"How about if you mistakenly describe her as the guy drinking a caffeinated beverage? After all, her hair is shorter than yours." Sheridan gives me a sour look. "Still referring to her?"

Sheridan nods. "I think so. Especially if you can see who I'm talking about."

"What if she's sitting very still and as a result you mistakenly refer to her as a mannequin? Are you still referring to her?"

Sheridan throws me a puzzled look. "Strange, dude. Very strange."

"I'm just trying to illustrate that there comes a point where your description is so far off that you fail to refer to the young woman altogether, though it is not entirely clear where that point is."

"What does this have to do with Zeus?"

"It's the same basic issue here. How wrong can we be in our description and still successfully refer to Zeus? You see, many early Christians actually believed that the Greek gods like Zeus existed, but not in the way the Greeks and Romans thought. The Christians believed that there were demons that corresponded to the specific gods. I don't know whether they were right to think that, but that's an interpretation of the existence of Zeus consistent with Christian belief."

"So you're saying that if Zeus really exists, he's a demon?" Sheridan asks, astonished.

"Not necessarily, but it's at least possible that there's a malevolent spirit being out there who has answered to the name 'Zeus' and who once accepted worship at ancient Greek temples. And if this finite spirit exists then we could say that Zeus does exist, but the Greek and Roman mythologies of the creature were wrong. In that case the Greeks may have been describing 'Zeus' with a range of descriptions that, though incorrect, were not so incorrect that they failed to refer to this demon being altogether."

Sheridan snickers. "So maybe 'Zeus' moved Katie's keys, too."

I shrug. "One thing I do know is that even if Zeus exists, he's not the most perfect being, and that's the only being worthy of our life's focus."

20

Would a Most Perfect Being
Have a Most Imperfect Church?

* * *

Fair enough, Randal," Sheridan replies. "I have no problem conceding that Zeus is not going to win the Best God to Start Worshiping prize. But what makes you think your petty tribal deity Yahweh is the most perfect being? Even if he exists, worshiping him seems like praising someone responsible for a whole lot of bad stuff."

"For starters, while Zeus was created by other gods, Christians and Jews always taught that Yahweh is the creator of all things."

"Oh, right," Sheridan replies sarcastically. "I forgot about that."

"Hey, you're the one who brought up Zeus. The difference between various concepts of God is important for eliminating certain descriptions of the most perfect being."

"Fine, if you seriously need a reason to exclude Yahweh from contention in the 'greatest possible being' contest, just look at the stupid things his followers do."

"To what are you referring exactly?"

Sheridan's countenance darkens. "Okay, Mr. Apologist, let me tell you about a case that I studied in a sociology of religion class. A ten-year-old girl from Perth, Australia, named Tamar Stitt was diagnosed with advanced liver cancer. According to the doctors, she would have had a 50 to 60 percent chance of survival if she would submit to a seven-week course of chemotherapy, but she'd have no chance of survival without it. The parents refused the treatment for their daughter, opting instead to pursue various so-called natural cures. As the weeks dragged on, her parents did nothing to help her. Eventually the hospital appealed to the Supreme Court in Perth to force the treatment she needed. The night before the case was to be heard by the court, the mother fled with her daughter to El Salvador so that Tamar could be treated for her cancer 'naturally' in accord with 'God's will.' You know what treatment they offered her? Drink herbal tea and put on mud wraps. All the while she was succumbing to her illness, a fate that would see her die by slow suffocation while her body was wracked by agonizing pain. How many people need to suffer because of Christian idiots like this?"

I can tell Sheridan is angry. While the case is undoubtedly tragic, to make matters even more complex I don't know enough about Sheridan to tell where Tamar's story leaves off and his own might pick up. "That is a terrible story," I say carefully. "But how exactly does that work against Yahweh's claim to be God?"

"Presumably if God is perfect, and he is going to establish a religion, then he will ensure that his followers in that religion are reasonable people. But as far back as you care to look your God has been trailed by an unbroken chain of idiots."

"Idiots? The whole lot of us?"

"I'm not saying all Christians are equally idiotic. But the ratio is uncomfortably high. It seems to me it's a lot higher than a really perfect God would allow. And anyway, how do you know Tamar's parents didn't read Yahweh's will correctly? Don't you believe that God directed Abraham to sacrifice Isaac? Didn't Jesus say that faith could move mountains? These kinds of actions are a direct result of one's beliefs about God. If there were a God, don't you think he'd straighten these morons out? Or is it part of his perfect plan that children suffer agonizing deaths?"

"I don't think those parents correctly understood God's will, Sheridan," I say gently. "I think they were deeply misguided to pit modern medicine against their untested cures. Medical quackery has nothing to do with the Christian view of God. In fact, this tragic story could just as well have been about a couple of atheist parents who favored quackery to proven medical treatments. I am not sure why you're blaming the Christian concept of God for the medical ignorance and foolishness of some deeply misguided parents."

"Atheists don't do stuff like that."

"Come on, Sheridan—where's your famous reliance on evidence? Now you're the one who's cherry-picking examples to support what you already think. Critics of Christianity often throw out such stories without establishing that Christianity makes people more prone to doing stupid or evil things."

"Of course they're more prone to act that way. I'm not about to misread God's will since I'm an atheist. It's only when you start thinking that there's an invisible sky God who may ask you to do things the world considers 'foolishness' that you get into trouble. And you've always got the perfect response, too. 'God's ways are higher than our ways,' right? 'All things will work together for good' for poor little Tamar, right?"

I shake my head. "I can see nothing about Christian theism that would predispose a person to trust mud wraps over modern medicine. Parents subject their children to abuse and neglect for all sorts of reasons, not just religious ones. Do you remember that guy in Colorado who fabricated the hoax that his son was trapped on a weather balloon in the hopes that he could get his own reality TV show? We don't blame reality television for that guy's poor parenting, do we?"

"Maybe we should. You Christians were happy to blame Ozzy Osbourne when some kid killed himself while listening to 'Suicide Solution.' So why don't you blame God for all the things his followers do? The fact is that belief in God promotes fatalism. Look how Tamar's parents were resigned to her fate from the beginning. By their twisted logic even popping an aspirin would have constituted a lack of faith."

"I disagree strongly with the parents' decision, but a fatalistic attitude has no more intrinsic connection with Christianity than does quack science. The Christians I know believe God works through modern medicine and that he expects us to use our common sense and the best technology. There's no essential link between theism and fatalism. After all, the old song 'Que Sera Sera' isn't a hymn. Tamar's case is terribly tragic and her parents' beliefs were tragically misguided, but it's unfair to tarnish all Christians with these sad aberrations."

"Unfairly tarnish? Christians are the ones doing these stupid things!"

"But how often do Christians do these things compared to non-Christians?"

"Read the headlines! You just don't read about atheist parents doing that kind of stuff. But there are lots of Christians who are like Dennis Rader. Remember him? The 'bind, torture, kill' murderer by night and an elder in a Lutheran church by day."

"Lots?" I reply incredulously. "For one thing, Christians outnumber atheists by multiple orders, so it's not surprising we'd have more examples of Christians committing evil acts—just like we have more examples of Christians committing heroic and good acts, by the way. How many of the hospitals and orphanages built in the last two millennia were built by atheists? And don't forget that the largest mass-murderer of the twentieth century was an atheist. All humans can commit great evil, Sheridan.

"Look," I continue. "Christians are easy targets when they do evil. Say a Christian and a secularist both kill their wives. The Christian killer becomes a big media story because he's a deacon and Sunday school teacher, but are the newspapers going to make a big deal about the atheist killer subscribing to *Reason* and belonging to Mensa? Nearly every Christian is a member of a formal organization like a church, so their actions tend to taint the entire group. Think of Christianity like a corporation with two billion members—the bad press from a tiny minority of its members is never-ending."

Sheridan looks unconvinced, as if I'm trying to explain away the actions of Tamar's parents. "I'm not trying to diminish the offense when Christians like Tamar's parents act foolishly or immorally," I say. "What they did was evil, and it ought to be punished—which is exactly what I'd say if her parents were atheists or followers of Zeus! I'm just saying we should keep those unfortunate actions in perspective. I certainly don't find that the sins and errors of individual Christians—or people who claim to be Christians—warrant the conclusion that Yahweh isn't God."

21

Would a Most Perfect Being Command Genocide?

* * *

Okay, Randal, I'm going to let you off that hook, but only because I'm about to hang you on an even bigger one. We could debate all day how much evil Christians have done and to what degree that undermines their claims about God. But it's not nearly the biggest problem anyway."

"So what is?"

"I had this Sunday school teacher, Mr. Benchley, who was on a mission to teach his flock of lambs all the hardest truths in the Bible. Unlike our other teachers, he didn't shy away from taking us through all the worst stuff in the Old Testament. I remember reading 1 Samuel 15 where the prophet Samuel, speaking on behalf of God, orders King Saul to kill all the Amalekites, including the babies. So how's this for irony, Randal? The same God who directs his righteous children to harass poor single women at abortion clinics to save American babies is steamed that Saul didn't butcher Amalekite babies. So what lesson should I draw from that? That a fetus's life is inviolable but babies can be bludgeoned on the divine say-so? Or maybe that Americans are more valuable than Amalekites? Do you think that a most perfect being would order the slaughter of infants?"

Rather than open my big mouth too soon, I decide to give Sheridan the floor for a while, since it looks like he still has a lot to say. "You know what Mr. Benchley said when I asked how a loving God could command the slaughter of infants?" Sheridan holds up three fingers and begins to count them off.

"One, 'God is Lord of life and death.' I still remember his squinty eyes peering at me through his coke-bottle glasses with that shrill, nasal voice: 'He's the Lord of life and death, Sheridan!' Two, he said the Amalekites were so sinful that they would have 'infected' the Israelites if 'God's people' had not completely wiped them out. How that's supposed to apply to infants I don't know. And three, he said that they had been given time to repent and they hadn't done so. God was merciful for a long time, but he had to let the hammer drop eventually, I guess. So they got what was coming to them. But when did the infants get a chance to repent? And while we're on the topic, what would an infant have to repent of?

"You know, Randal, you can talk about a perfect being who caused the universe to exist. Maybe that's true. But you can't seriously suggest that the Yahweh of the Bible is that most perfect being. He's more like a bloodthirsty barbarian."

"I'm definitely sympathetic to your point," I reply. Sheridan's expression shifts from aggression to surprise, and then to something bordering on smugness.

I continue. "If I were considering whether the deity of some other religion could be the most perfect being, I probably wouldn't go any further in processing his or her application if there were atrocities like that on the résumé. Which of us would consider a religion other than our own if it had a sacred text depicting its divine being commanding a holy genocide? For all Mr. Benchley's enthusiasm about the Bible, I bet he'd also reject without a second thought any other religion that attributed genocide to God."

"Right on, dude!"

"The fact is that many Christians struggle with this problem. I certainly do. When my daughter was younger, I purchased her first complete Bible. It was an 'Adventure Bible' replete with a jungle safari theme, cartoon mascot characters and the text rendered in a playful green font."

"Wow," Sheridan says sarcastically. "Nobody markets the Bible like evangelical Christians."

"When I first got the Bible, I paged through all the most horrifying problem texts, curious to see how this Adventure Bible dealt with them. I looked at Deuteronomy 20, which outlines the grounds for conducting a holy genocide, Joshua 6–11, which narrates the way the Canaanites were slaughtered en masse, and the text you mention, 1 Samuel 15, which refers to the slaughter of the Amalekites. In each of these cases God approved of or even commanded actions we would consider moral atrocities. We don't need the Third Geneva Convention's guidelines on treating prisoners of war to tell us that slaughtering infants and the elderly is wrong."

"So how did your kid's Bible handle these atrocities?"

"Let's just say it was underwhelming. I remember that the page with Deuteronomy 20 featured a green parrot with a factoid bubble that said Israelite men could be exempted from having to fight if they had been newly married, had recently built a home, or were just plain scared. That's of peripheral interest, I guess. But the question I figured most kids would be asking—how a perfect, loving and merciful God could command such moral horrors to begin with—was not even acknowledged."

"Green-letter edition, huh? Can you imagine if they sold a red-letter edition of the Bible?"

"They already do," I reply, doing my best not to laugh.

Sheridan looks at me shrewdly. "Not red for Jesus' words. Red for every bloody section. That'd make more sense. The 'Wartime Atrocity Bible.'" Sheridan laughs. "I gotta say, you're tripping me out here, Randal. I've never heard this from a Christian before. When I grew up in the church I was always told just to believe. Doubts were a sin, and questioning passages in the Bible was a one-way ticket to hell."

"Unfortunately, Sheridan, the fact is that Christians have typically handled the problem of violence in Yahweh's name much like the Adventure Bible does."

Sheridan smirks. "You mean with cartoon parrots?"

"With silence and peripheral distractions."

Sheridan lets out a low whistle and then adds, gloating slightly, "Well, I'm glad to hear you admitting the obvious."

"What's more," I say, "Christian apologists have often been no better than the laity at handling the problem."

"What? Now I'm really getting interested. Keep going there, Reverend. You're on a roll."

I shrug. "Look, I'm not here to defend the 'home team.' I'm only trying to pursue the truth as best I can, just like you. There's a lot of great stuff in apologetics these days on lots of topics like intelligent design, cosmic fine-tuning, the resurrection of Jesus and countless other topics. But it seems to me that the standard apologetic treatments of biblical violence and Old Testament genocide are very unconvincing by comparison."

"You're right on that, dude. Christians believe that their God is supposed to be infinitely more loving and just than any human being could ever be. And yet you also accept as God's authoritative revelation a book that depicts your deity commanding actions that would automatically be counted as moral atrocities by any decent person. No moral person today would dare justify the genocidal horrors of Nazi Germany, Khmer Rouge Cambodia or Hutu Rwanda. And yet I'm supposed to believe that genocidal butchery—

the savage slaughter of women, children and the elderly—is okay if your God commanded it. Come on. Talk about arbitrary!"

"You've got an unsettling way of putting things, Sheridan. I've seen a number of ways of dealing with the problem of biblical violence that end up misrepresenting the problem and thus misleading people about it. Probably the most common method I see apologists use is trying to justify the Canaanite genocide and other instances of Israel's battles as instances of just war."

Sheridan looks skeptical. "And what do you think a just war is supposed to look like, anyway?"

"Just war theory seeks to identify conditions that must be met for a war to be engaged in justly. For instance, there is the criterion of just cause, according to which a just war must be directed by a legitimate authority. In addition, the war must be undertaken as a last resort, and it must employ only the force necessary to address the threat and no more. Just war theory also allows for some collateral damage, including the death of civilians, but only so long as the civilians are not directly targeted. I'm sure I don't need to tell you that right-thinking people treat infants as civilians."

"Every war was just for Mr. Benchley since he thought all humans were garbage—his term was 'total depravity'—and thus it was just divine mercy that kept God from slaughtering the whole lot of us. But I remember my youth pastor giving me that just war line once. We had a question box at a youth retreat where you could ask the pastor anything. Most of the kids submitted questions about sex and dating like how far you could 'go' before it was a sin. Well, I asked about biblical genocide. And to his credit the pastor did try to answer. He claimed it was a just war, like you said. I even remember he compared it to the NATO bombing in Bosnia."

"That's not surprising," I reply. "The just war line of argument is common. Unfortunately, it's also deeply misleading as a defense of the Canaanite genocide for a couple reasons. First, just war categorically prohibits the targeting of civilians, but according to passages like Deuteronomy 20:16 and 1 Samuel 15, Israel was commanded to kill everything in the land, including the elderly and infants. Under no rule of just war could such carnage possibly be justified. Further, a just war can never be offensive—only defensive or retaliatory. But Israel's battles were clearly offensive. They invaded the land of people who did not want to fight them and who had lived on that land for hundreds of years."

"Okay, so it's not 'just war.' That's one strike against the apologists. What else?"

"A second popular line of defense is to explain that the genocide was a necessary reaction to a very wicked culture. The claim is that the Canaanites had to be wiped out because they were so debased that they even sacrificed their own children to Molech. God declares his hatred of child sacrifice in Leviticus 18:21 and 20:2 and Ezekiel 2:31 and 23:37."

"Yeah, I remember hearing how the Canaanites were so wicked that they just had to be wiped out."

"But there are at least two problems with that response as well. First, it's strange to punish a people for killing some of their children by killing all of their children and everyone else in the society, too. It's like punishing a shepherd for mistreating some of his sheep by killing his whole flock and family. It just doesn't make sense."

"Maybe the logic is like when a father punishes his son for smoking a cigarette by making him smoke a whole pack."

"Hmm, interesting analogy. Are we starting to reverse roles here?"

"Hey, man, I thought you might need a hand."

"I appreciate the goodwill," I say with a laugh. "Anyway, smoking is one thing, killing babies and undertaking genocide—those are very different. The Israelites are effectively saying, 'Since you just killed some of your people, as punishment we'll kill all of you.' And that doesn't make sense as a just response. But the problem is even worse since the Israelites viewed the slaughter as divinely sanctioned holy war, a pious religious act in which the Canaanites were considered *herem*."

"What's that?"

"*Herem* is a Hebrew word that refers to things being handed over to God for destruction as a form of offering. For instance, the word appears in Deuteronomy 20:17, where it's commonly rendered in English as 'utterly destroy.' The term signals that the whole act of war and killing was to occur in a religious context. The Canaanites were, in effect, human sacrifices that the Israelites were offering to their deity, Yahweh."

"Wait a minute. You're saying the Israelites punished the Canaanites for sacrificing people to their gods by sacrificing the Canaanites to Yahweh?"

"That's the basic picture. Needless to say, these events cannot be rationalized as battles gone awry like the American troops who massacred civilians at My Lai in Vietnam. As horrific as My Lai was, this was much worse because it was a premeditated religious devotional act. For the Israelites, the slaughter of Canaanites constituted human sacrifices to Yahweh."

Sheridan looks stunned. After a moment's pause he whispers, "Dude, I don't have words for how wrong that is."

"Of course, they weren't acting any differently from other ancient near eastern peoples. Everyone in the ancient near east was sacrificing their enemies to their gods. Talk about culture and geography—if you and I lived back then, we'd probably both be pro–'sacrifice our enemies to our god.' So the Israelites were no worse in that regard. But neither were they much better, which is what you certainly would have expected from a people who had been chosen by the most perfect being to be a light to the world."

"My point exactly. Evil is still evil, dude."

"There is one more major strategy that apologists often use to lessen the offense of these texts. They attempt to limit the conduct of *herem* killings to the period of Canaanite occupation in order to suggest that this activity was an exception for one specific period of Israel's history. According to one dating of the account in Joshua, that period of wartime occupation would have extended from around 1440 to 1400 B.C. But that narrow restriction of the *herem* cannot be defended since we find references to *herem* killings four hundred years later in that passage you mentioned where Samuel commands Saul to submit the Amalekites to the *herem*. And we can find hints of the *herem* even later in the Prophets. But we don't find any text that says unequivocally, 'Let it be known in all Israel that forthwith God revokes categorically and in all circumstances the practice of *herem* and all human sacrifice. Such actions are now considered absolutely abominable.' You have nothing like that. Instead, the evidence is that the practice slowly peters out—I suspect in part due to a growing moral embarrassment on the part of the Israelites."

Sheridan strokes his scruffy chin. "I don't get it. What's your angle in telling me all this? It's like you're Coke turning over your secret formula to Pepsi. If I were a Pepsi exec, I'd be suspicious."

"It's simple. What I'm saying is true. And I think Christian apologists could use a little more objective and rigorous exposition on this difficult issue."

"So what's your answer? Get a new Bible like Thomas Jefferson did? Maybe a little cut-and-snip until you have only the parts you like?"

"That's not an option for me," I reply. "Most often Christians tend at times like this to appeal to mystery. They'll say that even if we can't understand the justice of the actions, we should accept these accounts anyway."

"Right, isn't that the 'stop using your brain and just accept what I say' response? I've heard that one before."

"I wouldn't have put it like that, but I share your sense that the mystery response is inadequate here. You've probably figured out I'm not a big 'mystery' man."

We both smile and I continue. "To my mind, the problem is not merely that I fail to see how sacrificing babies can be morally praiseworthy or good. Rather, the problem is that I can see that it can't be good."

"Wait, say that again. Slowly."

"Sure, there are many cases where we accept something as true even though we're not sure how it could be true. Here's an example. Light photons seem to have the properties of both a wave and a particle. The physicist accepts this as true even though he doesn't know how it could be true. But I don't think sacrificing babies is like that. I don't think we simply fail to see how this could be good or praiseworthy. On the contrary, I think we can see that such actions can't be good."

Sheridan nods intently in agreement. I continue, "And I would add that, existentially speaking, I find the appeal to mystery very unsatisfying. I'm utterly incredulous about the idea of the Israelites being commanded by God to slaughter children in his name. I've read contemporary accounts of Christian Hutus 'righteously' killing Tutsis in Rwanda, and I have no doubt that they represent the depths of human evil. In my view, changing the Hutus to Israelites, the Tutsis to Canaanites, and 1994 to 1440 B.C. changes nothing morally speaking: evil is still evil."

Sheridan says, "I've heard that some Christians doubt the Canaanite genocide even happened. Instead they view those texts as ancient Israelite propaganda. What would you say to that?"

"You're right; some Christians do hold that view," I reply. "Many Hebrew Bible scholars interpret much of the Torah, Joshua, Judges, Samuel and Kings as largely nonhistorical, ideological literature that includes legendary folktales about the founding of the nation of Israel. Think of it as a mixture of straightforward myth like Paul Bunyan and his blue ox along with historically embellished legends like George Washington felling the cherry tree. If one takes that view of the texts, then one could argue that God never commanded these acts."

"So would you be satisfied saying that?"

"Personally I don't find any response to offer a completely satis-fying treatment of the moral and theological issues involved. You see, even if one took that position, I would still have the problem that the texts portray the Israelites as carrying out these acts under divine command. So then one can simply rephrase the question by asking why God would allow texts that portray divinely mandated acts of violence to come to be held as inspired and authoritative by the community of faith. In other words, dehistoricizing the texts merely shifts the problem from 'Why would God command atroc-ities?' to 'Why would God allow people to think he commanded atrocities?' Perhaps that's an easier dilemma, but it still is a dilemma."

Sheridan finishes his cappuccino and looks squarely at me. "Thanks for admitting that. Even if your apologetics are under-whelming, at least you're honest. But don't think that means I'm going to consider your God as candidate for most perfect being."

"I see your point since, as I said, I'd reject other religions and their holy books if they contained such atrocities."

Sheridan looks emboldened by this admission. "Darn right, dude. In fact, that's the only reasonable response. The fact is that you're grasping at straws at this point to sustain your faith. If you're not appealing to mystery and you're not sure about whether the events happened or not, then how do you resolve the problem?"

"Here's my view. Since I believe that Yahweh is the greatest pos-sible being, I must conclude that he did not actually command these actions. In other words, whether or not Israel actually slaughtered other ancient peoples in God's name, I do not believe that God commanded them to do it."

"Careful, buddy. At the church I grew up in, doubting any word of the Bible would have gotten you tarred and feathered."

"I don't doubt the Bible, but I do question how it's been inter-preted."

Sheridan looks impatient. "Just answer the question: Are parts of the Bible false?"

"No, I don't think so, as long as the Bible is properly interpreted. I'd say that while the human authors may have said some things that are in error scientifically, historically or morally, God nonetheless had a sovereign and perfect reason to include every detail. In the sense of divine intention there surely is no error."

Sheridan looks mystified. "Dude, I'm not really tracking with you. What is your view of the Bible then?"

"Let me give you an illustration. I recently picked up a book edited by Christopher Hitchens called *The Portable Atheist*. It includes writings by atheists, skeptics, agnostics and humanists from the ancient Greeks down to today. Does Hitchens agree with everything in all the writings he included in his book? Of course not. In fact he cannot, since on a number of points the authors included in *The Portable Atheist* disagree with each other. But that doesn't make him a bad editor; he had great reasons for including all these writings in his book. By analogy, we can think of the Bible as a divinely edited book in which God compiled the writings of dozens of human authors into a single collection. Here, too, every work that ends up in the collection belongs there—but that doesn't mean that every statement of every work is without error as per the human author's intention."

Sheridan looks amused. "Comparing Hitchens to God. Nice!"

"Thus, when there is apparent conflict in the Bible, we need to choose which of the voices in the text will be the authoritative one. For instance, if I have to decide between the Israelites who massacred their enemies and Jesus telling us to love our enemies, then I'll take Jesus."

"That's an interesting way to look at it, but why would God include morally offensive texts in the Bible to begin with?"

"God could have all sorts of reasons to include human works that have morally problematic dimensions within his work. Here's another analogy. Fyodor Dostoyevsky was a famous Christian writer who included in his novel *The Brothers Karamazov* some of the most powerful atheistic arguments ever penned as spoken through the character Ivan. You might wonder why a Christian would be the author of articulate arguments that he disagreed with profoundly, but that is to think too narrowly. The fact is that Ivan's voice serves the overall work. It could be that God included morally errant texts in the Bible to carry the story forward like Ivan carries forward *The Brothers Karamazov*. As I said, when there's a conflict between the genocidal Israelites and the Christ who calls us to love and forgive our enemies, I would see those violent texts as serving as a foil, a visible parable of human folly and sinfulness."

"But if that's the way the Bible is supposed to be read, then why has God allowed it to be misread for most of Christian history?"

"That may be the biggest problem with my proposal, Sheridan: It lacks a strong interpretive tradition. While I could say a lot more about that, for now I'm happy just saying that admitting this proposal as a possibility removes the objection that Yahweh cannot be the most perfect being because of biblical moral atrocities."

22

What Hath a Most Perfect Being to Do with a Most Horrendous Hell?

★ ★ ★

Sheridan looks a bit disoriented. "I have a feeling that understanding the way you read the Bible could be the start of a long conversation." He looks at his watch. "And that probably requires more time than I have. I guess maybe the Christian tent is a bit bigger than my experience."

"You may not agree with me on my reading of those moral atrocity texts, Sheridan. Certainly many Christians wouldn't. I'll be happy if you'll just concede that a person who sees these texts as an insurmountable moral barrier may be rejecting a particular reading of the texts rather than rejecting the God of the Bible."

"If you say so, Randal; I'm not going to bother arguing the point. Anyway, I'm not sure it really matters because I have another reason to reject Yahweh as the most perfect being."

Sheridan's voice gets softer. "My parents divorced when I was a kid. My dad was an alcoholic and my mom had finally had enough of his drinking, so she gave him the boot and married Mike. He's the Bible thumper who dragged me to church. My dad never did get his drinking under control, but he wasn't a bad man, you know? In fact, as far as dads go he was pretty cool. For my twelfth birthday he took me to an Iron Maiden show. You do know Iron Maiden, don't you?"

"The medieval torture device or the aging English heavy metal band?"

Sheridan chuckles. "For 'Brother Mike' they were the same thing. Even though Mike hated the 'devil's music,' my dad made sure I grew up listening to his favorite bands: Led Zeppelin, AC/DC and Iron Maiden. Every Friday he'd pick me up from school on his Harley and take me to Dairy Queen. He made me feel pretty cool. Not like Mike. His idea of getting crazy was hitting the speed limit in his minivan."

"So what happened?"

As I ask the question Sheridan gets a far-off look in his eye. Then his expression darkens. "When I was thirteen, my dad rode his bike under a semi and was killed. He was drunk. Mike said he had gone to hell because he lived a sinful life. No, wait, I think it was a 'debauched' life. Yes, that was the operative word. I remember looking 'debauched' up in the dictionary on the day of dad's funeral."

"Wow, what an insensitive jerk."

"Not really," Sheridan replies matter-of-factly. "He was just being honest. From a Christian view, my dad was 'debauched.' And as Mike said, the Bible is pretty clear on where debauched people like my dad end up." Sheridan pauses and then looks at me. "Unless you've got a way to get rid of hell, too?" The sarcasm from the quip leaves a chill in the air.

"Actually, Sheridan, that's another area that I've wrestled with for a long time."

Sheridan looks at me intently. "So what have you concluded? Do you think a God who is, as you say, the most perfect being would really damn some of his creatures to hell forever?"

"I think the first thing to note is that the Christian's response to hell has often been like the Christian's response to biblical violence: We tend to avoid the problem. In fact, avoidance is probably more common today than ever. Even a couple of generations ago you could count on the fire-and-brimstone revivalist preacher to wield the hot poker of eternal damnation as a way to stoke revival. But these days preachers are more likely to present Christ as a complement to a comfortable suburban lifestyle. And you sure don't want hell in that sales pitch."

"No, sirree." Sheridan grins.

"I've noted this trend in my own teaching at seminary. Every year I ask students if they can remember the last time they heard a sermon on hell. On average only about 5 percent can remember ever having heard a sermon on hell."

"Well, they didn't go to the church I went to."

"Actually, Sheridan, I think your brimstone church is kind of retro. Most churches dropped the topic of hell years ago."

"Why is that?"

"Some Christians take the disappearance of hell as evidence that we are 'capitulating to secular culture' and 'losing a sense of God's holiness.' I agree that describes part of our increasing discomfort with hell. And I think these are troubling trends. But I think there are other factors at play with which I'm more sympathetic."

"Such as?"

"I think that in many ways we are more humane, more morally sensitive, than people were in the past. There's lots of evidence for this. Two centuries ago, slavery, racism and sexism were all socially acceptable. I mean, women got the vote in many 'developed' Western nations only within the last hundred years. And the idea that we should treat animals with compassion has also only gained widespread assent within the last few decades. We still may be racist or sexist in our attitudes, but it is much rarer today to find those attitudes actually codified in legislation and social mores.

Generally speaking, these days we have to keep our baser instincts to ourselves. With that in mind, I suspect that at least some of our discomfort with hell results from a heightened perception of its morally problematic nature."

Sheridan looks amused. "Man, you should go on tour: The Self-Destructive Apologist."

"Maybe I could open for Iron Maiden? Anyway, in my experience Christians often treat the doctrine of hell in a way that parallels their treatment of *herem* violence: We either ignore hell or we misrepresent it. The fact is that the mainstream view of hell is actually a lot worse than most Christians, or even most skeptics, realize."

Sheridan shakes his head and chuckles. "Keep going—how's it worse?"

"For starters, insofar as there is a mainstream traditional doctrine of hell, it is properly described as 'eternal conscious torment': eternal because Christians have believed that hell goes on forever, conscious because it is believed to involve the sentience or awareness of the damned individual, and torment because it involves that individual being subjected to the most unimaginable agonies."

"Mike didn't put it exactly in those terms, but I think he said the same thing when he talked about the eternal lake of fire that sears flesh forever. He always described the flames as 'searing flesh.' I guess that sounds worse."

"Yikes, that's pretty gross. You know, as an aside, it's important to note that Christians have long disagreed over what it takes to end up in hell. At one extreme, some Calvinists have affirmed that even some babies end up in hell."

"Amalekite ones, no doubt!"

"Not necessarily. They'd say that it is up to God alone to decide which infants he saves and which he damns. Thankfully, most Christians haven't the stomach for that view. In recent years even the Catholic church has officially rejected the doctrine of limbo, which was for many years a popular belief among the laity."

"Limbo? What, the dance from Trinidad?"

"No, Sheridan, the other limbo, the region that many Catholics used to teach would be populated with all the infants who died without baptism. The fact that the Catholic church has officially repudiated the teaching on limbo and granted infants the possibility of full salvation is a good example of how Christian doctrines can change and develop through time. So on the destiny of infants, at least, there is a generous consensus. And that, it seems to me, is a great example of a more humane ethic positively shaping the development of doctrine."

"What about the fate of everybody else?"

"Once you get beyond babies, controversies rage. For instance, Christians disagree over whether you need to hear the gospel in order to be saved by Christ. Exclusivists say yes, but inclusivists say no. That is, inclusivists say that people who have never heard of Jesus and his atoning death can still be saved by Christ. In this view, people could put their faith in Christ without even knowing they're doing so, perhaps by responding to the general revelation of God in nature or through some other medium. Theologian Karl Rahner referred to such people as 'anonymous Christians.'"

Sheridan laughs. "I doubt the rabbi who teaches Judaism at the university would appreciate being called an anonymous Christian! Look, that's all interesting, but it's also pure speculation. Here's my question. I know my dad wasn't a saint, but he wasn't a Hitler either. I loved him, and he really did love me. He screwed up a lot, but he also tried to do his best with what he was dealt. So how could he deserve something as terrible as eternal conscious torment? How could anybody?"

"First off, it's important to recognize that Christians are not driven to their views out of hatred for others. Rather, they come to their views out of a conviction that this is what the Bible teaches. They don't relish the doctrine. They simply find themselves obliged to accept it."

"Don't relish it?" Sheridan looks skeptical. "Dude, I doubt that. Mike seemed to relish telling me about my dad's fate. I tried to argue with him a few times about it. Big mistake. He used Scripture verses like bullets, and his favorite topic was hell. Disagree with Mike? Bam-bam-bam! There goes the Holy Ghost machine gun."

"Okay, I should have said 'Christians ought not to relish the doctrine.' Not every Christian is the best ambassador for the Bible," I admit. "I'm just saying that there are biblical reasons why Christians believe what they do. It's usually not because they're closet misanthropes."

With this I pause and pull a Bible out of my bag.

Sheridan shakes his head in mock fear and looks over at you. "Oh no, better watch out, Reader. He's finally pulling out the big guns." He lifts the copy of Dawkins's *The God Delusion* and pretends to use it as a shield. Then he peeks over the cover and says, "I'll give you credit for your restraint, Randal. I'm surprised that it took you so long to whip out the ol' Bible."

"I think it's important to get some texts in view on this issue," I reply. "Here's Jesus speaking in Matthew 25:41: 'Then he will say to those on his left, "Depart from me, you who are cursed, into the eternal fire prepared for the devil and his angels."'" I close the book and turn to Sheridan. "Those are the words of Jesus describing a future state when he consigns the wicked to a fire which he describes as eternal."

"So how do you explain a text like that then? Was Jesus wrong? Was he also a victim of an unenlightened age? Or maybe Jesus is right and all you contemporary Christians just got mushy!"

"Maybe that's true," I reply. "In order to think this through we need to start with humility and an honest reflection on our moral intuitions. I'll tell you this much: the 'eternal conscious torment' reading of this text is definitely out of sync with contemporary notions of justice."

"What do you mean?"

"Well, consider contemporary theories of jurisprudence. These days, two primary rationales are given for punishing the guilty: reformation and deterrence. The rise of the view that punishment should be concerned with reformation is evident in the popularization of terms like 'correctional institute' and 'corrections officer' in place of 'prison' and 'prison guard.' Increasingly, jurisprudence is focused on reforming and restoring the offender. As for deterrence, there the rationale for punishment is to provide consequences that will dissuade others from engaging in criminal activity. So it makes sense to punish in order to reform and deter others from crime. You can probably see where this is going. Unfortunately, the judgment of hell fits neither of these rationales. The point of hell certainly cannot be reformation if the person is to be punished forever."

"Well that seems pretty obvious," Sheridan says. "But how about deterrence? Could you Christians justify hell as a deterrent? When I was being dragged to church we always had evangelists coming who'd try to 'scare the hell out of people.' I remember when I was like ten or eleven I smoked a cigarette with one of my buddies. His dad found out and told him that if he liked smoking cigarettes so much, God would let him 'smoke' forever! He never tried another cigarette. So his dad used hell as a deterrent from smoking. Maybe God will use an eternal hell as a deterrent from sinning to make sure that the saints stay on the straight and narrow."

"Sheridan, are you suggesting that God might damn some people to keep everyone else on the straight and narrow in heaven?"

"Hey, why not? Maybe God let my dad experience torment in hell to make sure Mike never sins when he finally gets to heaven."

I look at Sheridan closely but I can't tell if he's being serious. Perhaps he doesn't know how seriously his suggestion has been taken by some Christians. "Actually, some theologians have defended that view," I admit reluctantly.

"Oh, no, are you serious?" Sheridan sits up, a mixture of fascination and disgust on his face. "Dude, I was joking!"

"But I think that's a mistake," I add hurriedly. "It seems to me that there are severe problems with trying to defend the existence of hell as an eternal deterrent for those in heaven. First off, even if subjecting one person to eternal suffering would serve as a deterrent for keeping others from sinning, I don't think it would be just to subject someone to eternal punishment just for this reason."

"I agree. I read about this dude in Saudi Arabia who had his hand amputated for shoplifting. No doubt the threat of such an extreme punishment would be a powerful deterrent for would-be shoplifters. But even if the threat of amputation dropped shoplifting rates to zero, I still don't think it would justify amputating someone's hand for stealing a purse."

"Good illustration, Sheridan," I say. "That's one good reason to believe that hell couldn't be an eternal deterrent. And there are further problems with the idea. Consider the nature of heaven. According to Christian theology, people who are living in a glorified, redeemed state will not need a deterrent to keep from sinning since they will have become fully holy and no longer find sin appealing. In fact, they'll find the idea of sin completely repulsive. So it will not be possible for them to do evil. In addition, there will be no opportunity to sin since the environment will be perfect. So the morally perfect people that will populate the new heavens and new earth simply won't need a deterrent. And one more thing: even if God did require an eternal deterrent to keep people in heaven, surely he wouldn't need to subject real people to real suffering in order to secure the required deterrent effect."

Sheridan looks puzzled. "I don't follow you."

"Let me give you an example. Have you ever heard of 'hell houses'?"

Sheridan shakes his head. "Not sure what you mean."

"Every Halloween some large conservative churches stage a 'hell house.' It's basically an evangelistic alternative to the standard haunted house. The idea is that you walk through this house and look on scene after scene of the wages of sin being played out by actors. For instance, in one scene a young woman might be dying from a botched abortion, while in the next scene a drug addict is going through withdrawal. As you would expect, the hell house culminates with people suffering in hell. Christians stage these hell houses and file people through them because the shock value has a powerful effect."

"People get the hell scared out of them?" Sheridan asks with a grin.

"It looks that way. So here's my point. If the cheesy orchestrations of a suburban yuppie church with amateur actors and lame homemade special effects can be effective at warning people away from hell, imagine what God could do if he staged his own hell house. And he wouldn't even need actors. The whole thing could be virtual: every time you would even think about sinning, God could whisk you off to the virtual hell house for a 'debriefing' to remind you what's at stake. With a divine hell house there simply is no need for real people to suffer forever."

Sheridan looks puzzled. "So if hell isn't for reformation or deterrence, what's the point?"

23

An Eternal Eye for an Eye

* * *

Well, Sheridan, according to mainstream tradition the purpose of hell is ultimately retribution."

"Good ol' payback?"

"Basically, yes, although it's emphatically not the payback of the neighborhood loan shark. God's payback is perfect justice, not crass vengeance. I think we can all appreciate the intuitive appeal with the retributive notion of justice. Who doesn't think rapists or murderers deserve punishment for their crimes? Even if they could repent and be transformed in an instant, they'd still have to repay a debt to society. So then one could explain hell as a just retribution for sins for which the debt is infinite. In other words, the debt is an eternal punishment because the sins are infinite in gravity. Thus that's what damnation is all about. It's God's just payback on human sin and rebellion."

Sheridan nods. "I can see the logic of retribution. If someone does something terrible, like Hitler, then we don't punish merely to deter others and reform the offender. There's something about justice that requires punishment. So I get that."

Sheridan gets quiet for a minute before continuing. "But what did my dad do that was so bad, apart from drinking and swearing too much? He may not have been a saint, but he sure wasn't a devil. Every year he rode his Harley in Toys for Tots. He loved my sister and me, and he treated us the best way he knew how. And you know it wasn't exactly like he had a good role model. My grandfather was an alcoholic and he beat the crap out of my dad a lot. He also molested my dad's sister. My aunt still sees a psychiatrist because of that. Personally, I think my dad probably drank for the guilt of not protecting his sister from that monster. Doesn't all that baggage count for something? Maybe if you grow up in a shiny happy home you can become a good suburban Christian. But my dad's parental role model was an abusive pedophile. When you consider all the baggage he had to carry, the fact that he got as far as he did is pretty amazing."

I nod sympathetically.

"So, then," Sheridan adds sharply, "how could God just damn people like that?"

I take a deep breath. "Christians often explain the justice of hell by talking about how abhorrent sin is to God. We need to compare ourselves not to other fallible human beings but to the perfect standard of the God-man Jesus. If we do that we can see more clearly the justice of retribution in hell."

"You're saying that I just don't know how bad my dad really was?" I can hear the anger in Sheridan's voice.

"I'm not talking about your dad," I add quickly. "I'm talking about everybody: you, me, Mother Teresa, everybody. According to a Christian view of the fall, we're all in the same boat. Think of the human race as people living in abject poverty in a slum. If all we've known is the barest subsistence existence, we might think that getting 'cleaned up' is rubbing some dirty water on our cheeks, even though that does little more than smudge the dirt. As a result, we'd have no idea of the standards of personal hygiene required when we're invited to a royal state dinner. Only when we compare ourselves to the austere dignity of the king can we get a sense of how far we are in preparing ourselves for the standards of a state dinner. That's the way it is when you think about human beings coming into God's presence in eternity. Perfection is required of us, and we're all a very great distance away from it.'"

After a moment's pause I add, "So please don't get me wrong. I'm not talking about your dad. I'm just offering a general Christian analysis of the human condition. Every one of us faces the same dilemma."

"Look, I know what you're saying," Sheridan replies. "'For all have sinned and fall short of the glory of God.' Don't forget that I grew up in the church. But your analogy makes the problem worse, Randal. If a king invites peasants to a state dinner, shouldn't he ensure they're ready to go in if they don't know any better? That's on him! And even if I agreed that we all fall well short of perfection, that still doesn't make eternal punishment just. My dad may have died far from perfect, but that doesn't mean that he deserves a horrific punishment that goes on forever."

"I know what you're talking about, Sheridan. While I believe that part of our problem with hell is a failure to grasp our own sinfulness and God's holiness, there's still a huge leap to accept the justice of eternal damnation. In 1981 Dudley Wayne Kyzer was convicted in Alabama of a vicious triple homicide. His sentence was, for many years, the longest ever recorded in the annals of justice: two life sentences plus ten thousand years."

"Whoa, dude, that's long!"

"Yes, and Hitler's sentence, had he lived to face justice at the Nuremberg Trials, would presumably have been even longer. At least it should have been. But even the longest sentence of finite duration, even a sentence a billion trillion years long, is still only the first moment in eternity. So if it doesn't astound us to think of anybody facing an eternity of torment, we probably haven't reflected deeply enough on the horrifying nature of eternal damnation."

"So then what's your answer, Mr. Apologist?"

"Let me first note one point that Christians commonly make to justify the eternal suffering of hell."

"Don't tell me; let me guess." Sheridan begins to wag his finger as he says, "God doesn't send people to hell. They send themselves."

I'm surprised. "Sheridan, how did you know I was going to say that?"

"Ha, you don't grow up in a conservative Christian church without hearing that one, like, a hundred times. The problem was that I didn't see my dad shaking his fist at his creator. He always said he believed there was a God but that he found God on the open road, not in a church."

Sheridan looks at me and laughs. "Sounds cheesy, doesn't it? But I think he was being sincere. My dad didn't fit into angry fundamentalist churches, especially after he was burnt by a couple of them. He was actually asked to leave a church once because he was wearing a leather jacket and blue jeans. Not appropriate attire for the Lord's house, I guess. Okay, maybe he didn't meet the dress code, but does that mean he was shaking his fist at God? There just wasn't a church he could have fit into."

I take a deep breath. "Like I said, I'm not going to get into any speculations on your dad. Again, I'm sure that you know the basic response. God loves all people but some of his children choose to reject him. And God cares enough about his creatures to respect their free will and grant them what they wish."

"Correction, Randal. That's the Arminian story," Sheridan says. "Mike is a Calvinist, so don't go feeding him that 'free will' stuff."

Sheridan's use of these theological terms catches me off-guard. "Fair enough," I say. "For the Calvinist, hell is an even bigger problem since in that theology God could have saved all people but he chose not to. In the Arminian view things are very different: though it pains God greatly, he is forced to turn human creatures over to their own sinful wills."

"But how could anybody choose hell?"

"Maybe it's not as impossible as we initially think. It never ceases to amaze me how people can choose to engage in actions that they know will only make them miserable. Don't people choose hell-on-earth constantly, despite having the chance to choose something better? Addictive behavior is like that, whether it's a desire for cocaine or simply a curmudgeon's resolve to think the worst of people and allow bitterness to eat away his soul. We can secure our own misery by knowingly engaging in all sorts of self-destructive behaviors. Is it really impossible to think that these self-destructive patterns might become so entrenched that they could go on forever? From that perspective, maybe hell is an eternal self-chosen path of destruction: the ultimate self-imposed exile."

"It's that simple, huh?"

"Nothing's simple," I say emphatically. "But I do think this is at least a more plausible account of hell. It seems to present hell in such a way that God can be perfectly loving and good and still allow people to go there by their own free will."

After studying me carefully Sheridan observes, "But you don't look very convinced."

"Does it show?" I reply lamely. "Well, I have to admit that I see some very serious problems with the idea of a wholly self-imposed eternal damnation."

Sheridan looks at me intently. "Go on."

"For the sake of argument I'll concede that hell represents the natural consequences of people committing their lives to a destructive course. This may remove an objection to the justice of God, but it still raises critical issues about the love and mercy of God. In particular it leaves me asking, why would God allow people to continue putting themselves through such inconceivable agony? Imagine a young woman who in her self-loathing repeatedly cuts herself and burns herself with a cigarette lighter. We wouldn't let her keep doing that just because she wanted to. We'd restrain her if need be. We'd do all we could to stop her from hurting herself. If our compassion would go that far, why wouldn't God step in to stop the self-imposed suffering of his creatures? And if the only option were for God to, well, snuff people out of existence as a last resort, wouldn't he at least do that?"

"Amen," Sheridan says.

"We shouldn't forget that according to Christianity everything exists because God chooses to sustain its existence at every moment. So you might think that a merciful God would allow the hopelessly damned simply to lapse into non-existence, kind of like unplugging a lamp from the socket. But instead we're supposed to believe that God chooses to maintain these wretched creatures in their self-imposed state of agony forever as punishment. Why would an infinitely loving and merciful God do such a thing?"

"Good question, Mr. Apologist. The more we talk, the more you persuade me that I must be right."

I shrug. "Hey, like I keep saying, my job isn't to sell you a set of beliefs. I'm trying to present a rigorous and honest analysis of the issues and explain why, despite whatever difficulties might remain, I stake my tent where I do."

I pause for a moment and then continue. "There's an even bigger problem with this popular idea that hell is a fate the damned impose on themselves: That picture is just not biblical. I'm not denying that personal choice is an element of hell, but I am saying that this cannot be the whole story. The problem is that in the Bible hell is not described as a place where people are simply left to their own self-destructive choices. Rather, it's described as a place of punishment that God has set aside for the wicked. For instance, in Matthew 25:46 and Jude 1:7 God is described as preparing hell for the wicked and then sending them there."

"So," Sheridan says, "you're saying that God is in charge of building a giant damnation dungeon?"

"Er, that's an interesting way to put it," I say carefully. "There's something else that makes the picture look even worse. The Bible doesn't say simply that the wicked go to hell when they die. That's a popular misconception. Actually, it teaches quite clearly that there will first be a resurrection of both the saved and the lost. Obviously that's good news for the saved, but it means that the lost will be brought back to life with a new resurrected body precisely so they can be subjected to eternal suffering in that body. So it's not only that God preserves the damned in existence. Even worse, he actually brings them back to life to be objects of his eternal wrath."

"Now you're saying my dad was resurrected so that he could suffer in hell eternally?"

"First off, I'm not saying I know where your father is or where he's going. Anyone who tells you they know that is lying. Okay?"

Sheridan looks intently at me but doesn't say anything. I continue. "Second, according to the traditional doctrine nobody is in hell yet. In the Christian view, people do not get consigned to hell until after the resurrection, and the resurrection is a future event."

"Okay, right, so Dad isn't in hell yet. He needs to be resurrected in a new body first. Then he can be tortured eternally," Sheridan adds cynically. He looks at me darkly and says, "It is torture, isn't it?"

"Well . . ." I say with notable unease, "yeah, that's something you won't hear Christians come out and affirm very often. I've often heard Christians say that the damnation of hell isn't a form of torture, but it is. And that's not a controversial claim; it's simply a matter of definition. If you open a dictionary you'll find *torture* defined as 'the infliction of intense physical or mental pain for the purpose of punishment.' By that standard definition hell most certainly is torture."

"Okay, so then what is my dad going to be doing in hell? How will he be tortured? Will he really be seared in the lake of fire like Mike says? Or what?"

I can hear the pain in Sheridan's voice, and I throw a cautionary glance your way before answering. "I certainly cannot speculate on what hell will be like, although I take images like 'lake of fire' and 'outer darkness' to be metaphors of the suffering, not literal descriptions."

"Oh, just metaphors, huh? Thanks for clearing that up," Sheridan replies sarcastically.

"This brings me to a really important point. I need to stress that the traditional doctrine of hell as eternal conscious torment is not at the heart of Christianity in the same way that Jesus, the Trinity and atonement are. What I mean is that you could reject the doctrine of eternal conscious torment and still be a Christian."

"How so?"

"You could take another view of hell. Even if eternal conscious torment is the traditional Christian view of hell, there are other views—minority reports, you might say."

"And what are those 'minority reports'?"

"There are two main ones. To begin with, there is annihilationism. This is the view that after the resurrection those who are not in relationship with Jesus will be destroyed."

"Like capital punishment, you mean?"

"Basically, yes."

"Why think that's anything other than wishful thinking?"

"There are many texts that speak of the future destruction of the wicked. For instance, Jesus warned in Matthew 10:28 to be aware of the one who can destroy both body and soul in hell. There's no talk there of people being sustained in fire. Rather, the picture seems to be that the fire ultimately destroys them."

"And that's better because . . . why? It's more merciful?"

"Absolutely it is! Think about the difference between eternal conscious torment and simply disappearing. God does not force his will on anybody. He allows people to make their own decisions. Perhaps we could even think of this punishment as something like euthanasia: that is, as a relatively good and merciful death for people who have rejected God."

"So now God's like Jack Kevorkian, the suicide doctor? But don't forget that you mentioned a resurrection. Kevorkian never brought people back to life just to kill them again. So why would God bother to resurrect people? Just so he can try out new modes of capital punishment? Why not let them stay dead and just be done with them?"

"That's a valid question. It may be that the answer lies somewhere in the mysteries of divine justice. I'm still studying this issue, believe me—remember, I'm not known as the mystery man! But at the very least, this view presents fewer problems than eternal conscious torment."

"So that's it, then? My dad will be resurrected either so he can be pitchforked like a shish kebab on the heavenly barbeque or so he can be mowed down by an angelic firing squad?"

"I have to hand it to you, Sheridan. You've certainly got a way of putting things."

"Well, I don't think hiding behind Hallmark catch phrases is appropriate when you're talking about my dad's fate."

"You're right about that. And whatever else can be said about our conversation today, I'm thankful for your honesty—it inspires me to be as honest and forthright as I possibly can. But like I said, there's one more minority report. It's called universalism."

"Universalism?" Sheridan looks at me in surprise. "Like where everybody is saved?"

"You're right; it's the view that everybody will be saved. Some Christians believe it to be a heresy—but other Christians disagree."

"I assume universalists can claim their set of Bible texts, too?"

"Yes, they can. Texts like Colossians 1:20, Philippians 2:11 and Romans 5:18 can be read as teaching the ultimate reconciliation of all creatures to God. So for example, Colossians 1:20 states that God is reconciling all things in earth and heaven to himself through Christ's blood shed on the cross. The plain reading of this passage seems to teach universal reconciliation. There are only two ways to avoid that conclusion. The first is to argue that some people are reconciled to God by being damned in hell, but that's a pretty strange way to be reconciled. The other is to say Paul is exaggerating here because not everything is actually reconciled. That isn't very appealing either."

"Does that mean that people don't really need Jesus? God will save you anyway?"

"No, that's not the view. Rather, the view is that the saving effect of the atoning death of Jesus will eventually extend to all people."

"But what about all the hellfire texts?"

"Biblical universalists don't deny hell—they only deny that it is forever or final or always populated. According to universalists, hell is ultimately intended for the reformation of God's creatures to bring them to the point of repentance and transformation."

"The restorative logic of punishment, huh? I dunno. I always heard universalism being referred to as a heresy when I was growing up." Sheridan laughs. "Brother Mike would be having fits right now if he heard you calling it a 'minority report'!"

"In the interests of full disclosure, Sheridan, I don't share the convictions of the universalist. But I know evangelical Christians who do uphold the inspiration of Scripture and the atoning work of Christ and who also believe that Christ's atoning death will win out eventually and restore all creation to God. And they have biblical and theological reasons for holding their view."

"But you don't buy the universalist's pie in the sky?"

"No, not exactly," I admit, "but neither do I dismiss it altogether. I find some middle ground by calling myself a hopeful universalist."

"Come again?"

"Let's say that you buy a lottery ticket and there are a million-to-one odds that you'll win. Given the odds it makes no sense to believe you will win, but does it make sense to hope you'll win?"

"That's a no-brainer. Why else would you buy the lottery ticket? You think there's a chance that you could win and so you hope you do."

"Right. Okay, so as I look at the evidence of the Bible that can be invoked in favor of universalism, and as I consider the minority universalist witness of the church tradition and the theological and philosophical considerations that support it, I find the arguments at least possibly true—even if not likely true. That is, I'm left saying that it is at least possible that God's love will win out eventually and save all people. It may only be a million-to-one shot. Or maybe the odds are better than that. I'm really not sure. But I think there are enough hints to let me rationally hope that all people will be saved."

"So you hope we all win the salvation lottery?"

"Sort of like that. And why shouldn't I? God is the most perfect being, so if anyone could accomplish this feat it would be him. And once I recognize that it's possible that everyone will be joyfully and perfectly saved forever, how could I hope for any other outcome? I mean, which Christian would want to see other people damned?"

Sheridan bursts out laughing. "Dude, you never met Mr. Benchley."

24

Three Types of Relativist and Two Types of Evil

* * *

Sheridan, I hope it's pretty clear that I don't mind talking about difficulties that I face as a Christian. I certainly sympathize with your moral indignation about the notions of divinely commanded genocide and eternal conscious torment. But I'd like to explore the nature of your indignation from your atheistic point of view."

"Fine with me, dude. I'm always up for a good cross-examination."

"It seems to me that your moral criticisms of Christianity are rooted in a deep sense of justice, mercy and goodness. Correct?"

"I think so," Sheridan replies.

"You clearly believe that it's always wrong to engage in genocide and subject people to eternal torture."

"No doubt."

"But where does the sense of absolute justice and goodness that drives your objections come from?"

Sheridan suddenly brightens. "Oh, now I see where you're going with this. You want to make the old 'If there is no God then every-thing is permissible' argument, right? Since I clearly don't think everything is permissible, you think I should believe in God." Sheridan laughs and looks at me condescendingly. "You're not seriously going to dust off that old fossil, are you?"

"I'm impressed at your apologetic literacy," I reply with an admiring nod. "That argument comes from Dostoyevsky's *The Brothers Karamazov*. And would you look at that?" I say with a broad grin, "I happen to have a copy right here." As I reach into my bag, Sheridan looks on with a mixture of disbelief and suspicion. "In one famous scene, Smerdyakov says the following to Ivan the atheist . . ." I start to read in my best Russian accent, which, as you can guess, is not too great: "'I first thought that if I had some money I could start all over again, either in Moscow or, better still, abroad; I got that idea, sir, mainly from "everything is permitted"—it was you who taught me that, sir, because you used to say it a lot—because, if there is no eternal God, then there is no virtue and, what's more, absolutely no need for it.'"[7]

I close the book. "According to Smerdyakov, Ivan claimed that two things followed from the non-existence of God. First, there would be no objective virtue or goodness, and this would free us to construct our own sense of goodness and to devise our own set of goals and rules to live by. With no divine moral oversight we can live as we please. But not only is there no virtue. Smerdyakov adds that there is also no need for virtue. He doesn't make clear what he means by this, but I suspect he means that there is ultimately nobody to reward or punish us based on how we have lived our lives. In that sense we're doubly free: free to make up our meaning and free not to worry about any posthumous settling of accounts because we made the 'wrong' choices.

"I think this is a very plausible line of argument," I continue. "It's extremely difficult to conceive of objective goodness and virtue existing without an absolute personal standard as their source. Since I find the evidence that objective goodness and virtue exist overwhelming, I conclude that this provides strong evidence for God's existence. To put it another way, if there were no God, then the most powerful people would effectively become the most 'righteous.' So if there is no human being more powerful than Genghis Khan to call him to account, then Khan can do what he likes while on earth. He could live as he likes because after death, that's it. If the winners write the history, they also write the moral code. What would you say to that, Sheridan?"

"Yawn. Another fossilized argument from the master of archae-ological apologetics. With no God we're left with 'might makes right'? Come on, Randy. You want us to wait for some non-existent sky God to settle the accounts in the next life? It's our job to visit justice on the Genghis Khans and Adolf Hitlers of history. The real problem is your view that says, 'Don't worry! Sky daddy will punish them so let's go along with their tyranny for now.'"

"I didn't say we shouldn't resist evil, Sheridan. Where did that come from? From a Christian perspective the kingdom of God is all about seeking justice. My argument is that we need God as the ob-jective source of the moral goodness and justice that we all recognize."

Sheridan shakes his head. "Sorry, I'm not convinced by that claim that we need God for the good. That's completely unnec-essary, like positing a bowling alley in heaven to explain the roll of thunder. We have a simpler, natural explanation of thunder. And we have a simpler, natural explanation of morality. We don't need to invoke mystical truths."

"Okay then, Sheridan, what's your account of morality and value?"

Sheridan moves to the edge of his seat and adopts an instructive posture. "Morality," he says, "is simply a species-specific aspect of our evolutionary history. It describes the proper way human beings ought to interrelate as human beings."

"Oh, now that's interesting," I say. "So you're actually a moral relativist?"

"Not at all," Sheridan replies indignantly. "I don't believe that morality is relative to culture, as if the Nazis had their morality and we have ours. I consider what they did wrong. And I certainly don't accept an individualistic relativism that says good and evil are decided by the individual. Your two Russians, Ivan and Smerdya-whatever, are completely wrong on that point. I believe that morality is objective to the species. It's simply part of our evolutionary history. Had we evolved in a different way we'd have a different morality. But this is the way we evolved."

"Fine," I say, "so let me make sure I have your position right. We have a species-specific morality that's a product of our evolutionary history. Consequently, had we evolved differently, then our morality would be different. Is that right?"

"Yeah, it's an empirical fact. Have you ever seen the morality of mice and rats? They eat their offspring. You don't think that's a different ethic of parenting?"

"Actually," I say, "I wouldn't call that behavior moral or immoral."

Sheridan looks at me strangely. "So what would you call it?"

"Calling the behavior of rodents moral or immoral is a category error since they're not moral agents to begin with. A mouse eating its young is not a case of moral evil but rather of natural evil."

"What's the difference?"

"Moral evil involves an intentional action by a moral agent to commit an evil action. Natural evil is evil that does not result from the intentional action of an agent. I don't believe animals are agents. So when creatures—animals or human beings—suffer and die because of events like earthquakes or forest fires or because of the action of a non-moral agent like an animal, then it's a natural evil. If a bear mauls a human, it's not trying to be evil—no moral agency, in other words."

Sheridan looks intrigued. "So let me get this straight," he says. "A man kills another man. Moral evil. A lion kills a man. Natural evil. A man dies in a fire set by an arsonist. Moral evil. A man dies in a fire started by a lightning strike. Natural evil."

"Yes, that'd be my view."

"And how do you know that animals are not moral agents?"

"A moral agent is an individual who is capable of distinguishing the moral value of actions and choosing to perform or refrain from other actions based on that moral knowledge. Sharks, bears, lions and mice are not capable of doing this. They're driven by instinct, not the moral assessment of actions. A cat that plays with a mouse for an extended period of time before eating it is not being cruel. Rather, it cannot experience compassion because it is not a moral agent. As for your view, Sheridan, you're claiming that when a species reaches a particular level of evolutionary complexity it evolves a morality, and in some cases creatures have evolved a morality in which it's good to eat their young. Is that right?"

"Yeah, that's just a fact. Although I don't know at which point animals began to evolve morality. I'm pretty sure that snails and spiders are not moral, but then maybe they're moral in their own way. If certain actions contribute to the flourishing of the organism or the species, then I'd say that the action is good for the organism or species."

"All right," I say, "so then you really are a relativist about morality. While you reject individual-relative and cultural-relative morality, you accept species-relative morality."

"Huh. I guess if you use your terms that way, then that'd be correct."

25

Good Humans, Genocidal Aliens and Serial Killers Who Know What They Want in Life

* * *

Ⅰ'd like to explore your view," I say. With that I reach into my bag and pull out yet another book, a paperback by Philip Carlo on infamous serial killer Richard Ramirez.

Sheridan looks on in astonishment. "Dude," he says in disbelief, "why don't you just get a Kindle?"

I smile. "That would be easier to carry around." I hold up the book and ask, "Do you know Richard Ramirez?"

Sheridan thinks for a moment. "Wasn't he some kind of murderer like Charles Manson?"

"Yes, Ramirez raped and killed close to thirty victims before he was caught and sentenced for his crimes in 1985. Ramirez is infamous for the great relish with which he recounted his heinous deeds. For instance, he once said . . ." I look down at the book and begin to quote: "I would shoot them in the head and then they would wriggle and squirm all over the place and then just stop, or I'd cut them with a knife and watch their face turn real white. I love all that blood."[8]

Sheridan looks at me suspiciously. "I hope you're not going to blame atheism for Ramirez."

"Wouldn't think of it, Sheridan. However, I want you to consider carefully what Ramirez said at his sentencing. He addressed the court as follows: 'You don't understand me. You are not expected to. You are not capable. I am beyond your experience. I am beyond good and evil.'"[9] I solemnly close the book and look up. "Now I have a question for you. Do you think it's possible that Ramirez could be correct, that he could really be 'beyond' the ethical norms of our species?"

"See, I knew you'd try that one. I already told you, Ramirez is evil and what he did is evil. It's that simple, dude."

"Not so fast. You said that you have a species-relative morality. My claim is simply that your view is inadequate to explain our moral intuitions. In your view an action that would be evil for Homo sapiens might be morally permissible or even praiseworthy for a creature of another species. Correct?"

"So what?" Sheridan raps his fist on the table like he's knocking on a door. "Hello?" he says, presumably intending to check if I'm home, mentally speaking. "Dude, Ramirez is a human being last I checked."

"Sure, for all we know," I reply. "But is it possible that Ramirez evolved beyond the species? Maybe he experienced some mutations in his genetic code when he was conceived and he is the first of a new subspecies for which the actions he committed are not moral horrors. In your view it's possible that actions that would be evil for a human being with human DNA could be moral for a creature with Ramirez DNA."

Sheridan puts his face in his hands, apparently to illustrate his disdain for my argument. Nonetheless, I persist. "Look, if mice can 'morally' eat their babies, then perhaps a creature more highly evolved than us can rape, torture and murder human beings in accord with their interests. And if this is possible, then it could be the case with Ramirez. If a person happens to have Ramirez DNA, then rape and murder might be okay for them. That's the implication of your view, and it seems to me to be a serious problem. The mere possibility that Ramirez DNA could introduce a radically new morality is, in my view, sufficient to show that your species-relative view of morality is inadequate."

Sheridan looks up. "I'm not interested in what's possible. It's possible that I could get hit by a purple meteorite at any minute. But I don't worry because it's not plausible, it's not likely to happen. Your scenario isn't remotely likely either." Sheridan pauses. "In fact, I'm not even willing to concede that it is possible. I don't think that the kind of genetic advance that would be necessary for that kind of radical moral change could occur in a single person who otherwise looks like any other human being. The leap that would be required would simply be too great."

I shrug. "Maybe, maybe not. But it seems to me, Sheridan, that you have a problem. On the one hand, you have a strong moral intuition that certain actions are always, absolutely wrong. It seems to me that that intuition was driving your critique of biblical genocide and the doctrine of hell.

"However, when we turn to your view of what morality actually is, your account is too weak, too namby-pamby, to explain the strength of your intuitions. You want to say unequivocally that what Ramirez did is, indeed *must* be, absolutely wrong. But then you have to qualify this conviction by admitting that it depends on the assumption that Ramirez is fully human, because if he isn't, then maybe what he did wasn't so bad after all. It seems to me that you should let your moral intuitions take the lead here and concede that morality really does transcend the species—and thus that irrespective of whether Ramirez is fully genetically human, his actions were still morally heinous."

"No way, Randal. I don't see any problem here at all. My moral intuitions are human ones, so of course they're absolute for me.

And whatever fanciful possibilities you want to suggest about Ramirez's DNA, as far as I'm concerned, that's just science fiction. The reality is that he is human."

"You don't like sci-fi, eh? That's ironic since you're the guy who mentioned the idea of aliens creating the universe. How about we consider some real sci-fi? Did you see the film *District 9*?"

"Nah. It's like a parable or allegory about apartheid, isn't it?"

"That's part of it. In the movie, aliens come to Johannesburg, South Africa, in 1982 on a giant spaceship."

"Interesting. I thought aliens always arrived either on the White House lawn or in New York."

I laugh. "Maybe this is the exception that proves the rule. Anyway, the spaceship hovers over the city for months doing nothing. Eventually humans board it and discover a million aliens slowly starving to death. The poor wretches are subsequently removed from the ship and herded into a massive camp called 'District 9,' which is essentially a giant prison. There they're treated terribly and derided as 'prawns,' a slur that refers to their distinct resemblance to the delectable crustacean."

"'Delectable'?" Sheridan makes a face. "Ugh, speak for yourself. I hate seafood."

"Fair enough. Let's agree to disagree about prawns. But as for the aliens, they are highly intelligent and have their own culture and language. Though they're very different from us, they clearly are moral agents. This raises some pretty interesting ethical issues. For instance, in one scene an alien is callously being used by the human beings as target practice to test alien weaponry. Is that action of subjecting a sentient, and very terrified, alien to being blown apart morally permissible simply because the creature is not human?"

"No," Sheridan says with indignation, "of course not. It doesn't matter that the alien is not human. Our human morality doesn't allow us to treat any other creatures with that kind of wanton abandon."

"Okay, now let's reverse roles. Is it possible that the aliens might have evolved so that they could morally abuse and exploit human beings at their will? Is it possible that the so-called prawns might have evolved so that for them it is perfectly moral to rape, torture and kill human beings for entertainment? I mean, this isn't that crazy, is it? We eat beef burgers without a second thought because it gives us pleasure. Perhaps these 'prawns' evolved in such a way that they can morally rape, torture and murder human beings for their pleasure and personal fulfillment."

Sheridan looks dubious. "I'm not sure. I think you always get into trouble with science fiction because you can imagine anything. There's no control on the imagination."

"But the existence of aliens is a real possibility. So then if we put an alien like this on trial for the rape, torture and murder of a human being, that alien could conceivably deliver Ramirez's line to the court: 'You don't understand me. You are not expected to. You are not capable. I am beyond your experience. I am beyond good and evil.'"

Sheridan shrugs. "Highly evolved aliens who morally rape human beings? Yeah, I guess that's possible. Sure, why not? Lions and sharks eat human beings and we don't consider them immoral for doing so."

"But there's no evidence that lions and sharks are moral agents. However, the aliens certainly are since they have language, culture and technology. And yet you're agreeing that for them rape and other morally heinous actions could be okay."

"Earth to Randal," Sheridan replies. "We don't know if there are any aliens out there to begin with."

"It doesn't matter whether there are aliens or not. We're dealing here with what our moral intuitions say is and is not possible. My view of morality is that it is necessarily wrong for moral agents to rape, torture and kill other moral agents simply because it gives them pleasure. I believe the wrongness of these actions transcends all species, regardless of how they evolved. You seem to be suggesting that a sufficient change in our DNA could make torture a moral good."

Sheridan looks completely unmoved. "That'd hardly be the first time our intuitions have misled us."

"But Sheridan, I don't see any reason to think our moral intuitions are flawed about something so basic as the necessary evil of raping moral agents for pleasure. Perhaps it might help if we approach the issue from a slightly different direction. Are you familiar with the concept of 'convergent evolution'?"

"Sure. That's the process where creatures from unrelated lineages evolve the same biological traits. It's like when a marsupial shares a bodily form or trait with a mammal even though the common evolutionary ancestor of these two creatures lacks that form or trait. Like the marsupial squirrel glider bears a striking resemblance to the North American flying squirrel even though the common evolutionary ancestor they share would bear no visible resemblance to either."

"Good example! So selective pressures in the environment guide the evolution of organisms down a limited set of paths, and as a result very different organisms can end up looking very similar through completely different evolutionary histories."

"Yep."

"With that in mind, is it possible that there could be creatures that have a completely different evolutionary history from human beings but that, through the pressures of convergent evolution, have come out looking indistinguishable from human beings, much like your two squirrels?"

"Now that's some really fanciful science fiction."

"Maybe they even walk among us as we speak," I add. I wiggle my fingers and make an eerie "Twilight Zone" sound. "Perhaps it sounds crazy, but nonetheless it is possible. That means that it's possible a serial killer like Richard Ramirez could be an alien who evolved through convergent evolutionary processes to look like a human being. And that means it's possible that Ramirez's courtroom declaration was correct, that he really is beyond our morality and thus is free to rape, torture and murder human beings with moral impunity."

Sheridan is starting to look a bit exasperated. "You just don't get it. You can make your stories as wacky as you want, but that won't make them even remotely plausible."

"I think you're missing my point. The plausibility of the scenario is not relevant to the argument. Rather, the fact that this is possible shows us that your account of morality is insufficient to ground the absolute and unqualified nature of our moral intuitions. I'm saying that Ramirez's statement could not possibly be true, irrespective of whether he is a human being. No matter who or what he is, his actions are absolutely evil.

"Considering that," I say, "your species view of morality must be wrong. Good and evil apply to all moral agents, whatever their evolutionary history. Even if Ramirez evolved differently, it would not change our moral judgment one bit. We'd still count his actions as evil."

Sheridan is leaning back in his chair and rubbing his eyes. "This still sounds like science fiction to me, bro. Maybe you should start your own religion like L. Ron Hubbard did. You could invent your own alien mythology and call your followers 'Randalians.'"

I ignore Sheridan's quip. "So then if you had an alien Ramirez, you'd say that we shouldn't judge him?"

"I don't know about 'judging.' But it certainly would make sense to restrain him, just like you'd restrain a vicious lion. If he engaged in behavior that was natural and good for his species, who are we to judge him? It may not make sense to judge him, but we certainly could stop him in accord with human interests."

"You're a tough nut to crack, Sheridan. Okay, I'm going to push this thought experiment to its logical conclusion. Imagine that these humanoid Ramirez aliens evolved in such a way that on their planet certain acts like genocide of their own kind were morally praiseworthy. On their planet, one subgroup of their species called 'Joobs' were eliminated by a ruling party called the 'Mazis,' who rounded them up into concentration camps and gassed them. While the Joobs were destroyed under the false pretense that they were a threat to the wider society, this action ultimately had positive social benefits for the aliens as a species. You see, thinking that the Joobs were a threat that had been effectively eliminated provided a huge psychological boost to the wider population. As a result, the aliens as a species are now thriving as never before. Can you say that what happened to the Joobs was necessarily wrong without knowing something of the alien DNA and evolutionary history?"

"On second thought, Randal, maybe you shouldn't start your own religion. You could do a lot of damage making up stories like that."

"Come on," I reply impatiently, "just answer the question. Obviously you agree that the Nazi genocide of the Jews was a moral horror. But if you're saying that it is only a species-relative horror, isn't it possible that the Mazis' elimination of the Joobs could have been an expedient social policy to further the flourishing of that species?"

"I don't think that makes any sense. Changing DNA doesn't suddenly leave you with human beings who have a completely different set of species-relative moral values and obligations."

"Hold up, Sheridan. We're not talking about human beings at all. We're talking about a distinct species. Through the pathways of convergent evolution they may look identical to human beings, but they're still a distinct species. That's it. Just as you can have a marsupial and a mammal that look very much alike but are internally very different, so we have Homo sapiens and our humanoid aliens, externally indistinguishable but internally very different. The problem is that a species-relative analysis of morality means that rape, cannibalism, torture and genocide could be moral goods for the

Ramirez humanoid aliens, even though these actions are morally evil for real humans. Since this is highly counterintuitive, the thought experiment counts against your species-based analysis of morality."

"Bah," Sheridan says as he waves his hand dismissively. "I still think you're reading way too much science fiction. That's not concrete reality."

"Sheridan, repeatedly intoning about 'science fiction' is a red herring. Not only are your views implausible as descriptions of morality, but they also wreak havoc with our sense of moral progress. Right now we humans strive—in word if not always in deed—to achieve certain ends like courage, justice, patience and kindness. Your view entails that depending on the way our evolutionary trajectory progresses, there may come a point where we have to rethink and even abandon these virtues. More to the point, there may come a time when they are no longer virtues for us. Perhaps in the future it will become morally praiseworthy for a more fully evolved humanoid descendant of ours to rape and torture other creatures. Perhaps Ramirez is a glimpse into our moral future when the most morally virtuous of us are those who can rape and kill without conscience. That's possible in your view. But in my view, that fluid notion of moral progress is falsified by our very absolute moral intuitions. We know that certain actions and behaviors are always to be cultivated and others always to be avoided regardless of the future evolutionary direction of our species."

"Like when you rejected the morality of sacrificing babies?"

"That's right, Sheridan. The view of morality you've presented is very different. Despite all your talk about objectivity, your view of morality is actually highly relativistic, and for that reason I think it should be rejected.

"And," I add with the hint of a wink, "if that means you ought to consider becoming a theist, then so be it."

26

Playing Games with Morality

✶ ✶ ✶

Sheridan shrugs. "So long as we don't run into your raping Ramirez aliens, I think we'll be fine. I prefer morality that's grounded in empirical reality, not the philosopher's ivory tower imagination. Maybe I can explain it this way. Morality is objective just like the rules for a game are objective. The bottom line is that if you want to win the game then you have to follow the rules. If you want to be happy and live a long, fulfilled life, then you shouldn't lie, cheat, steal and so on. Morality simply describes the rules by which individuals and the species flourish. And I can't see any species flourishing if it acts the way you describe. Any species of raping Ramirez aliens and Mazi tyrants would die out pretty quickly."

"Well, don't tell that to praying mantises, Sheridan! It seems very possible that certain actions we might consider evil could, on balance, lead to a species flourishing. Carnivores have thrived for eons by eating other creatures without regard to their suffering. One could argue that many human societies have thrived while engaging in acts that we erroneously believed to be immoral, including human sacrifice, cannibalism, slavery and so on."

"But not in the long run," Sheridan insists. "Evolution takes lots of time—something a lot of science-denying Christians just don't grasp."

"How long does the run have to be before your claim is shown to be false?" I retort. "I think your conviction here is just evidence of your absolute moral intuitions. Let's look at it this way. If ethics is like following the rules of a game, then what's the goal of the game? Human flourishing and widespread happiness?"

"Something like that."

"Okay, and so we call those behaviors that help us win the game 'moral.' Correct?"

"That's right. If I violate the rules of the game, I won't flourish. If it's a serious enough violation I could end up dead or in San Quentin Prison. We act morally because it's the best way to ensure our own happiness."

"Personal happiness sounds like a pretty low, self-interested approach to morality, if you ask me," I reply. "And here's another problem: I don't think there's any universally agreed-on concept of human flourishing. Perhaps if there were we could claim that morality is the set of practical wisdoms necessary to achieve those goods that we all desire. But we don't all desire the same things."

"I don't think we're all that different," Sheridan replies.

"How about Armin Meiwes?"

Sheridan looks at me closely. "I don't know who that is—and I'm not sure I want to."

"You're probably right," I reply. "Armin is this German guy whose idea of winning the game of life included eating another human being. So he placed an ad on the now defunct 'Cannibal Café' web forum looking for another person willing to be butchered and eaten so that he could fulfill his lifelong wish."

Sheridan puts his head in his hands. "Dude, what is it with you? Do you stay up late at night trolling the Internet for examples from the dregs of humanity that you can use in apologetics debates?"

"Sadly, you don't have to look hard to find horrifying stories like this," I say. "They top the headlines. Anyway, Armin got his wish. He met up with another fellow in 2001 whose idea of winning the game of life was to be cannibalized, just so long as he could be mutilated before being killed and eaten. Needless to say Armin was happy to oblige. So in the end both of these guys got exactly what they wanted. It was a perfect exchange."

Sheridan holds his stomach. "Please, spare me the details or I might lose my rhubarb muffin."

"The bottom line," I say, "is that Armin made a calculated, rational decision based on the ends he wished to achieve. Following his own practical wisdom, he found another consenting adult whose rules and goals for winning the game of life fit his like a hand in a glove. So who's to say these two didn't win the game of life with respect to their chosen rules and end goals?"

"There you go again, Randal, still trying to paint me as a relativist, huh? Look, if you can say Tamar's parents are the unfortunate exception, why can't I say the same here?"

"The difference is that I have an objective reason to say Tamar's parents are mistaken. But you don't have any objective reason to say Armin was mistaken. Who says that the rules you and I hold are obligatory for all human beings? For you to adopt a subjective game view of morality and then deny that Armin's end goals in the game can be legitimate is flawed reasoning. Who says you make the rules?"

"Dude, we're playing the same game. You can't change the rules just because you want to!"

"Wait a minute, Sheridan," I reply. "Who says we're playing the same game? Maybe Armin is playing a different game of flourishing than you and I. Why do you think he needs to play your game? Only if you take a truly objective view of morality that says there is a certain set of values for winning the game irrespective of what any individual or species think can you truly ground an objective morality."

"I assume that you're going to say that Ramirez was playing another game as well?"

"Based on your view, why not? Armin played in accord with the rule that you should respect the wishes of the other person. Presumably that's why he sought a willing subject rather than just clubbing some poor bloke in a back alley. But who says the rule of 'willing consent' must apply to every game of human flourishing? It doesn't seem to be a rule in Ramirez's grisly game."

"Why do you Christian apologists always have to go for the most extreme examples? Most of us agree on the basic rules of the game."

"Those who disagree with our rules to the extreme that Armin or Ramirez do may be few and far between, but they are there and that presents a serious challenge to your view of morality. In their view, they just want to play a different game, and you cannot say objectively that our game is better than theirs. Besides, psychos who make the headlines aren't the only ones to disagree on what constitutes a good life. Often that disagreement may coexist comfortably within societal norms, but it is no less troubling for that reason.

"For example, consider the twin brothers Simon and Sherman. Simon becomes a human rights lawyer, selflessly fighting for indigenous peoples against the oppressive exploitation of corporations. Meanwhile, Sherman makes a living off an Internet porn site he started in his basement. In his free time he lounges in front of a big-screen TV, drinking beer and eating chicken wings. Most of us are inclined to say that Simon chose a superior game to Sherman. But in your view of morality all we're really saying is that we prefer Simon's rules and goals to Sherman's. What we can't say is that Simon's game is objectively better. We may prefer it like we prefer mint chocolate chip, but if Sherman prefers pistachio, who are we to judge?"

Sheridan looks thoughtful. "To be honest, there's something to what you say. I know guys at the frat house who would prefer Sherman's game. And I know guys in the business school who have a different game altogether: accumulate money and power and possessions."

"Good observation. You said a few minutes ago that we act morally because that's the best way of securing our own happiness. That leaves you with little more, morally speaking, than ethical egoism."

"Which is?"

"Ethical egoism says that we ought to act so as to maximize our own personal interests. But this isn't only a counterintuitive notion of the ethical life—it could be used to justify truly heinous acts, depending on what one's interests are. And you don't need to go to the extremes of a Ramirez to find an example. Imagine that Sherman the pornographer sees a miserable old coot passed out in an alley with a wallet stuffed full of money. Sherman can call the old man an ambulance, or he can just take the money and disappear into the night. Since the money could buy a lot of beer and chicken wings, he takes the man's wallet, thereby securing his own happiness. Given your criteria this could be a moral act. But surely that's wrong."

"I agree," Sheridan says.

"Ironically, Sheridan, the most curious part of your view concerns what it implies about God."

"What's God got to do with it?"

"You were adamant just a short while ago that no perfect being could command genocide or allow hell."

"Right . . ."

"But how can you sustain that objection? By definition, God is separated from human beings by multiple orders of difference. If you assume that other creatures can have a different morality than human beings—moralities in which actions like murder, cannibalism and rape are morally acceptable—then surely God could have a completely different morality. If that's the case, what basis do you have to use human morality as an argument against Yahweh being God?"

I pause, and when Sheridan still hasn't said anything after a few moments, I continue. "You know, the same problems arise when it comes to atheistic views of meaning."

"Meaning?" Sheridan retorts. "Isn't meaning just what you make it?"

27

God Is Dead and You Have Killed Him, Et Cetera

★ ★ ★

I smile. "Meaning is what you make it, eh? Well that's an interesting perspective. Remember I said that when you reject God you don't just reject God? You reject other things as well?" Sheridan nods. "Well, now we see the full implications of that rejection. By rejecting God you also reject both goodness and meaning."

Sheridan shakes his head. "That's what you say, but I think it's sad that you have to find meaning by visiting a church to worship an imaginary sky daddy."

"Now that I think of it, perhaps being an atheist does have some significant advantages. For one thing, you don't have to get up early on Sunday mornings to corral the kids in a frantic effort to make the church service on time."

Sheridan smugly tips an imaginary hat. "You betcha."

"Yup," I continue, "you're free to laze around the house, reading the Sunday paper while lingering over a cup of smoky French roast." Sheridan nods, gloating. "And," I add, "there's no requirement to give to the poor."

Now Sheridan gives me a strange look. "If the Christian kept the money she spends every month in tithes, in no time she could have a huge new television in her living room. And while the Christian groans under the weight of her lifelong obligation to do justly and love mercy, you're free to go play tennis, ride a bike or do whatever you like. That's not too shabby!"

Sheridan crosses his arms. "Hey, you don't have to be a smart-ass. Anyway, I agree with you, dude. I'd rather enjoy a cup of good coffee than sit on a hard pew in some stuffy church and listen to a two-bit preacher tell me how bad I am. As for tithing, you're seriously going to fault me for not wanting my hard-earned money to go toward paying off the mortgage on some drab building so that needy people have a place to delude each other? That's pathetic. And your assumption that because I'm an atheist I should care only about material stuff? Now that's really insulting. Maybe you're obsessed with getting new TVs, but I don't even own a TV. I'm more interested in giving my money to Oxfam and Amnesty International."

"I'm glad that you're into supporting worthwhile charities. I wasn't suggesting that atheists are or should be driven by materialist concerns. In fact, that's the problem."

Sheridan looks incredulous. "What are you talking about, dude?"

"In an atheist view of the world, there are no absolute 'shoulds' or 'oughts': no concerns necessarily take priority over any others. Ultimately all people are free to make their own meaning, just like Smerdyakov. That's the downside of all your autonomy. You have to give up the notion that there is any objective prioritization of choices for constructing meaning. No choice is objectively better than any other."

"Randal, you're simply out of touch with reality," Sheridan snaps. "I don't need to pretend I'm the handiwork of some sky God to find meaning in my life. I find meaning in the small things. Believe me, there's no God-shaped hole in my heart."

"But my point has nothing to do with whether you perceive a need for anything. The crucial question is whether atheism has the resources to provide objective meaning for our lives—something more substantial and lasting than whatever happens to turn one's crank at the moment."

"Don't worry, Reverend Randal. Like I said, my life is full of meaning and significance. Stop trying to make a problem where none exists." Sheridan looks frustrated. "You want meaning? That cup of coffee and morning paper that I enjoy while you're driving to church are a great place to start. What's wrong with finding meaning in a cup of coffee rather than communion wine? Maybe you find meaning in an insipid potluck in the church basement, but I prefer inviting friends over for dinner and wine. When it comes to meaning, my cup runneth over."

"How very King James of you, Sheridan. Look. I don't disagree that you can construe all sorts of things as subjectively meaningful. You find meaning in having a friend over for dinner? So did Armin Meiwes."

"Oh, come on," Sheridan says with indignation. "That's a cheap shot and a really bad pun. Cannibal jokes are not kosher, man."

"Yeah," I reply. "I admit they're in bad taste."

Sheridan looks aghast. "Dude, stop. You're just digging a deeper hole!"

"Okay, enough jokes," I say. "But the point remains. Since you deny a personal cause to the universe, you're committed to the view that human beings came from nothing, by nothing and, most importantly, for nothing."

"Yeah, we weren't created for anything. But so what? We're chance byproducts of a random evolutionary process. We don't have a purpose written into our genes. We don't have a soul to steer the ship. No angels to light the way. No pot of gold at the end of the rainbow. No—"

"I get the point, Sheridan."

"I'm glad. It seems that repetition is the only thing that might get through to you."

"And such poetic repetition, too!"

"But don't miss the point. None of that prevents us from making our own purposes. Each one of us has to write our own story. And the fact that some sicko writes a cannibalistic story just isn't of much interest to me. That's a story that the rest of us aren't interested in writing, thankfully."

"So you're saying that even if there is no objective meaning or purpose to human lives, we're still free to make our own meaning? We can build our own conception of a meaningful life?" Sheridan nods. "But is that a sufficient account of meaning? Is it adequate to say simply that we all 'write our own stories,' with the addendum that hopefully not too many of us write stories of cannibalism, rape or serial murder?"

"Dude, I think you already squeezed all the juice out of that orange with your Ramirez aliens."

"I'm not so sure. This idea that we must project our own meaning onto the universe reminds me of Timothy Treadwell. Have you heard of him?" Sheridan shakes his head. "Well, he was what you might call a classic eccentric. But the nature and genesis of his eccentricity are what make him interesting. For a number of years he spent his summers living among the Kodiak bears of Alaska. During his time with the bears, Treadwell and his girlfriend, Amie, filmed hundreds of hours of footage, some of which was incorporated by award-winning German filmmaker Werner Herzog into a fascinating documentary called *Grizzly Man*."

Sheridan perks up. "Herzog? The atheist director? Respect."

"Glad you like him," I reply. "As you watch Treadwell's erratic and obsessive behavior in the film, you're left to wonder what it was that drove him to spend his summers risking his life living with wild bears. Herzog gives his own analysis of Treadwell's motivations, which I find to be quite profound. He suggests that

Treadwell realized that his comfortable life in Southern California was empty. As a result, he set out on a sort of quasi-spiritual quest to find meaning in a romanticized conception of nature, what Herzog describes as the 'secret world of the bears.' In the view of Herzog, who as you noted is an atheist, the search was futile because in his view there is no meaning to be found in nature."

With that I reach into my bag and pull out a DVD copy of the film that I slot into my laptop. "DVDs, too?" Sheridan says. "Do you have any Iron Maiden CDs in there?"

"Unfortunately no," I reply. "But I do have Barry Manilow's *Greatest Hits*."

"Er, I think you better just play *Grizzly Man*."

As we watch footage of a bear filmed by Treadwell, we listen to the voiceover narration of Herzog:

What haunts me is that in all the faces of all the bears that Treadwell ever filmed I discover no kinship, no understanding, no mercy. I see only the overwhelming indifference of nature. To me there is no such thing as the secret world of the bears, and this blank stare speaks only of a half-bored interest in food. But for Timothy Treadwell this bear was a friend, a savior.[10]

I pause the scene and turn to Sheridan. "Herzog was right," I say. "That same bear that you see looking so bored in the footage was the very one that ate Treadwell a couple of hours later. Herzog recognizes that this tragedy provides a powerful metaphor for the human dilemma without God. We need meaning in our lives—and if there is none, if ultimate reality is indifferent to our existential plight, then we'll tend to project meaning onto the universe in an attempt to make meaning where none exists. But this is tragic self-delusion since, whether we end up being eaten by a bear or dying old and full of years, either way our fate is to be food for worms."

Sheridan looks unimpressed. "Bah," he says with a wave of the hand. "Treadwell was obviously mentally disturbed. Healthy people don't need to run into the wilderness. And I think Herzog's playing it all a bit too melodramatic for his material. He was obviously reaching for an Oscar."

"Maybe," I reply. "Or maybe he and Treadwell are playing the role of the madman in Friedrich Nietzsche's famous parable."

"Oh yeah, what's that?"

"It's a famous story Nietzsche told to describe the cataclysmic implications of rejecting a theistic view of the world. In the story, a man with a lit lantern runs into a crowded marketplace crying out that he is seeking God. Everyone in the village begins to laugh and taunt the man, chiding him by saying things like, 'Oh, did you lose God? Maybe he's hiding.'"

Sheridan cuts in. "Oh yeah, yeah, I remember reading that. Then the madman turns to the crowd, smashes his lantern, extends a quavering finger and declares, 'God is dead and *you* have killed him!'"

"Yes, that's right. And then follows what I think must be one of the most poetic passages in all philosophy." With that I lean over and pull out a copy of Nietzsche's *The Gay Science* from my bag.

Sheridan sighs resignedly. "You really do have everything, dude." I throw you a smug sidelong glance and begin to read the great German philosopher's haunting words:

> How could we drink up the sea? Who gave us the sponge to wipe away the entire horizon? What were we doing when we unchained this earth from its sun? Whither is it moving now? Whither are we moving? Away from all suns? Are we not plunging continually? Backward, sideward, forward, in all directions? Is there still any up or down? Are we not straying, as through an infinite nothing?[11]

I turn back to Sheridan. "That's the reality of a godless universe as Nietzsche sees it. And Herzog's analysis isn't much different.

There is no meaning or purpose in the world to guide our lives or restrict which stories are good ones since there is no 'good' to judge our stories beyond our own particular preferences. From this perspective, Treadwell comes out looking like the so-called madman of Nietzsche's parable. Though he looks crazy, he may be the only sane man in the village because he's the one who realizes that without God, everything changes. So it isn't that you just believe in one less god than I do. Without God, everything changes: morality, meaning, everything."

"You know, Randal, I'm beginning to think that maybe you're just wrapped too tight. We have all sorts of meaning without God. I find meaning in watching sunsets and in learning stuff in the seminar room and in going to the pub with friends after finals. You're trying to make it sound like we atheists lead lives of quiet desperation, like we're Richard Cory in Robinson's poem, putting on a façade but always teetering on the edge of suicide. I bet you feel vindicated every time an atheist kills himself because then you can say it supports your thesis."

"No way, Sheridan. My point has nothing to do with whether or not atheists are more or less well-adjusted than the general population. Whatever the psychological makeup and character of atheists, my argument is that atheism can't provide the metaphysical ground for the objective meaning that we recognize does in fact exist and that imbues our lives with significance and direction."

"How about helping little old ladies across the street? Is that meaningful enough for you, Mr. Christian?"

"For me? Yes, I believe that a life spent helping little old ladies across the street is objectively more meaningful and valuable than a life spent pushing them in front of buses. But in your view the difference is merely a matter of taste."

28

What Does God Taste Like?

* * *

Sheridan laces his hands behind his head and leans back in the chair. "I agree that helping little old ladies across the street is better than pushing them in front of buses. But I'm not sure I can make sense of the idea that it is objectively more meaningful. And even if I did agree with you that there is a God who establishes morality and meaning, I'd still be light years away from saying that Jesus loves me and has a wonderful plan for my life. Like I said, you always seem to paint the bull's eye around the arrow after the fact. When some evidence comes up against Christianity, you just tweak your doctrines enough to keep the old-time religion going."

After a pause, Sheridan adds, "There are thousands of religions, so I can never even begin to assess which one is true, or more likely to be true. And even if I did arrive at the view that Christianity might be true, I'm still left wondering which Christianity. How could I ever be sure that I've got the right one?"

"That's a big dilemma," I reply. "But it's misleading to pose it as a problem only for those who adopt a religious perspective of the world. Every one of us must consider what reason there is to take our particular view of the world over other views, whether the view we hold is 'religious' or not."

"Sorry, Randal, your *tu quoque* responses are getting tiresome. Just try addressing your dilemma for once."

"My dilemma is your dilemma," I insist. "You think there's only one 'scientism' or 'secularism'? Or that you've considered all the nontheistic ways to live?"

"Fine," Sheridan sighs. "Here's a way of putting it that's particular to you. How do you know you're tracking with the most perfect being in your religion? How do you know that Islam or some other major historical world religion doesn't have the real revelation of God? I don't have that dilemma since I don't believe in any revelation to begin with."

"Okay, that's a fair question. In response, I'd say that even though believing the right doctrines about God is important, there's something even more important."

"Which is . . . ?"

"It's more important to know whether we're in relationship with God than to know that we believe the right things about God. To put it another way, the most important question is not 'How many correct propositions do I believe about God?' but rather 'Am I in a saving relationship with God?'"

"Are you saying that you can believe all sorts of false things about God and still be in relationship with him?"

"Of course—you could definitely know God relationally while getting many facts about him wrong, just like any real relationship. The question is how one knows God. There are two different ways of knowing something. The first is propositional knowledge—the kind that's purely intellectual and that can be readily put into factual statements and shared with others. The other kind is what philosophers call the 'knowledge of acquaintance.'"

"'Knowledge of acquaintance'? Uh oh!" Sheridan says. My mystical baloney meter is starting to go off. You're not going to try protecting your beliefs by saying they're based on some kind of mystical experience, are you?"

"I assure you, I'm not going to appeal to any facts that are not widely available in one form or another to all people. Remember when I described the neurologist who knows everything about espresso from a third-person perspective? He knows everything about its chemical composition, the process of its manufacture and its effects on the human brain." Sheridan nods. "Well, that's propositional knowledge. Propositional knowledge is very important. But there's another kind of knowledge you can have of espresso, the kind that comes with actually tasting it. The knowledge of coffee that Mr. Dreadlocks has is knowledge by acquaintance.

"We constantly distinguish propositional knowledge and knowledge of acquaintance," I continue. "For example, you might know 'on paper' what a winter spent in Yakutsk, Siberia, is like because you've read extensively on the subject. You can discourse for hours on average snowfall, temperature, humidity, wind chill, hours of sunshine, available amenities and so on. But actually experiencing a Siberian winter? Well, that would give you a very different type of knowledge."

"I get the idea. Mike used to say that after I graduate I'll have to enroll in the 'school of real life.' I guess that's his way of saying that the propositional knowledge you get in university is very different from the acquaintance knowledge you get after graduation."

"The same distinction is relevant when we're talking about God," I reply. "We can have all sorts of propositional knowledge of God without the relational knowledge of acquaintance. But as I said, the more important kind of knowledge is knowledge of acquaintance. As the psalmist says, 'Taste and see that the LORD is good.'[12] It's certainly possible that we could be getting a whole lot wrong in terms of propositional knowledge while still being in a profound relationship with God—just like a child can get all sorts of facts about her parents wrong and still be in a profound relationship with those parents."

"So you're saying that thinking the right things about God really isn't that important? I can't believe I'm hearing this from a theologian!"

"Of course it's important. But the end goal of religious life is to be in relationship with God, to enter into that deeper and more profound knowledge of acquaintance. Long before the child has any true beliefs about the parent, the child is in relationship with the parent. On this point I'm with the inclusivists. Head knowledge is important, but it's even more important to have that knowledge of relationship."

"So what do you look for to show that you're in relationship with the numero uno?"

"Just as you can't provide any certain, definitive argument that there is no God, I can't provide a certain, definitive argument that I am in relationship with God. But I think Christians can identify reasonably good grounds or evidence that we are in this kind of relationship. For starters, I'd say that we ought to look at evidence in our own lives, evidence that we're becoming more Christlike. That is, we should seek evidence that we're becoming more generous, loving, forgiving and all those other things that the apostle Paul called the fruit of the Spirit. I'd say that the more Christlike we appear in our lives, the better the evidence we have that we're enjoying a relationship with God. To take an extreme example, the fact that Dennis Rader tortured and killed people in the evenings provides pretty good evidence that his daytime Lutheran faith had no relationship."

"Glad to hear it," Sheridan says sarcastically. "But I'm surprised you didn't mention praying a sinner's prayer."

"I think prayers of repentance can be an important step, Sheridan. And please don't misunderstand me as saying that people are saved because we do a certain amount of good works. I think our salvation is a matter of divine grace, from first to last. But the evidence that divine grace is working in our lives is found in our works—in other words, in what our relationship looks like."

"But what about others? Muslims? Hindus? Even atheists like me? What if a non-Christian looks 'Christlike'? Do you think they're in relationship with God?"

"I don't think it's my place to say how far God's grace might extend. In Matthew 25, Jesus tells a parable in which the sheep and goats are distinguished with respect to their works. This doesn't mean the works saved the sheep, but the works serve as signs of the genuine sheep."

"Okay, Randal, good works. I'll check that box because I'm a pretty good guy. Maybe I'm already in relationship with the God I don't believe in!"

I can tell Sheridan is trying to get a reaction out of me. And so, biting back my professor's tongue, I sit in silence so we can think.

29

The Light Cast by Little Amazing Moments of Providence

★ ★ ★

After a long silence, Sheridan begins to speak again. "Okay, so a lot of good works mean someone's probably saved, right?"

I wince at the bluntness of the statement. "That's not quite what I said. But I did say that good works can provide evidence that one is in relationship with God. I also think that God sometimes provides more specific signs of his benevolent concern for and involvement in our lives."

"Signs?" Sheridan asks quizzically. "Like what kind of signs?" He stares at me for a few seconds and then rolls back in his seat. "Oh, no, you're not going to pull out the old religious conversion stories, are you?" He begins to imitate a southern evangelist. "'He touched me, and I was never the same! Oh, hallelujah!' Stuff like that? Because excuse me if I'm skeptical, but Brother Mike loved dragging us to hear the good old gospel preachers. He's a good Calvinist with a holiness streak. I think all those preachers had the exact same testimony."

"Listen, Sheridan," I say emphatically. "You have a thing for treating people you don't agree with as objects and caricatures. I'm not talking about evangelists who work the crowd into an emotional frenzy just before they pass the offering plate. I'm talking about the experience that real, everyday people have of God working in their lives, and specifically how that working is corroborated when suggestive events occur. When this happens I think we can take these events as signs that God is real."

"I think I know what you're talking about," Sheridan says with a snicker. "One of my favorites is the old 'Footprints' poem." He starts to speak in a weepy grandma voice: "At the end of the beach of life I looked back and saw that at the worst moments there was one set of footprints. I thought the Lawrd had abandoned me, but no! That's when he was carrying me!" Sheridan raises his arms. "Puh-raise Jeeezus!"

"Wow, Sheridan," I say. "You do that quite well."

"I just wanted to spare you the trouble," Sheridan replies tersely.

"Thanks a bunch, buddy. But remember, I'm not interested in mere anecdotes or Christian kitsch or stereotypes. I want to bring some rigor to the discussion. On this point I think it would be helpful to begin with the criteria that William Dembski has articulated as prerequisite for justifying a design inference in scientific enquiry."

"Oh yeah? And what are those, exactly?"

"Dembski notes that whenever an event occurs we can attribute it to chance, necessity or design. I think this is as true in mundane affairs as in natural science. In fact, we already touched on this when we talked about the mysteriously moved keys. Remember we said that the moved keys could have had a personal agent cause or an impersonal event cause? The personal cause is tantamount to design, while the impersonal cause is tantamount to chance or necessity. You and I can call any synchronous event that arises from chance or necessity a 'coincidence.' So our question is whether a suggestive event arises from coincidence or design."

"Like what?"

"Some years ago I was driving along when the Michael Jackson song 'Don't Stop til You Get Enough' popped into my head, so I started singing it."

Sheridan starts laughing. "I would've thought a theologian like you would be singing George Beverley Shea."

"Anyway, a minute later I turned on the radio and the song was playing! At the time the song was more than twenty years old and not in heavy rotation, so it wouldn't have been played often on the radio. And I assure you I'm not a big Michael Jackson fan, so it was unusual for me to be singing one of his songs. Needless to say, it was very unusual to find the same song that had just popped into my head also playing on the radio. But—and this is a big 'but'—as unusual as this experience was, it lacked a meaningful signature, so I chalked it up to coincidence."

"Well, at least we agree on that," Sheridan replies.

"But in other cases a synchronous event happens that has a suggestive signature or pattern." Sheridan looks at me blankly. "Like a sign. It seems to mean something to the person who experiences it. If the pattern is sufficiently suggestive, a person can conclude that it's more than coincidence. There may be some intelligence superintending the event."

"Uh oh," Sheridan says. "Here comes God, huh? A TV pastor is being investigated for tax fraud, so when Michael Jackson's 'Beat It' comes on the radio he decides to flee the country!"

"Nice one! But let's not get ahead of ourselves. Often when suggestive, synchronous events occur, we invoke a human agency. Let's say that it's your birthday and your girlfriend asks you to stop in to buy some pizza at your favorite restaurant before heading over to her place."

"She'd never do that, dude. She's a vegan."

"Okay, your favorite Vietnamese vegan restaurant, then. When you arrive you find that the place is filled with balloons that spell out 'Happy Birthday, Sheridan!' Now that's a situation that cries out for a design explanation, because it has high complexity and a suggestive pattern or signature. In this case, the reasonable assumption is that a human being—most likely your girlfriend—was behind the greeting.

"However, it's at least possible that a highly complex event with a signature like this could occur and not be attributable to another human being. In that case you might invoke a divine agency. I call these synchronous events 'little amazing moments of providence.' For example, remember when I gave the example of a man lost in the woods who prayed for a sign to guide his way? Immediately after his prayer a meteor flashed across the sky and guided him out of the woods. That would qualify as a little amazing moment of providence."

"Little amazing . . . wait, 'LAMPs'?" Sheridan laughs good-naturedly. "That's kind of cheesy, dude. I thought you weren't one for Christian kitsch."

"How about I promise not to market my LAMPs acronym on calendars or coffee mugs? It may be cheesy, but I still say it's appropriate and descriptive. These events are 'lamps' because they cast a light into our lives, letting us know that God is at work and that we're on the right track."

"But how can you possibly justify attributing these events to God? It's one thing to say a human being did something, but it's another thing to say it was God. Isn't this just another god of the gaps? What if science explains the event?"

"Actually, I don't see any problem with an event that occurs by scientific necessity also being a lamp."

"Wait a minute. I thought you just said that you can infer a designing mind behind the event only if the event is not a matter of chance or necessity."

"That may be Dembski's view, but mine is a bit different. In my view, the causality of the event is not as relevant as the strength of its signature."

Sheridan shakes his head in bewilderment. "I don't think I follow you. How could an event that has already been explained, perhaps even predicted, in accord with scientific laws, still qualify as a 'lamp'? What's left for God to explain?" Sheridan snickers. "Does Noah's rainbow qualify?"

"The rainbow? No, unfortunately. But I can give you another scenario from meteorology. Let's say for the sake of argument that the current view that weather systems are inherently unpredictable is shown to be false. As a result it becomes possible to predict future weather events with certainty up to one day in advance. Let's imagine further that these one-day forecasts become so accurate that they can predict with certainty not only that it will rain but also the future trajectory of every raindrop, snowflake or hail pellet up to a full day in advance. Finally, let's imagine that weather.com offers custom forecasts of tomorrow's weather for your city, neighborhood—even your own backyard. All you need to do is go to the website and type in the coordinates of your house and you'll receive a completely accurate backyard forecast for the following day. One day you get the forecast for your backyard because you're planning an outdoor birthday party for the following—"

Sheridan looks indignant. "You're putting me into another birthday illustration?"

"Fine, it's your annual celebration of the day you first met me at the Beatnik Bean!"

He laughs and I continue. "So a second later the forecast pops up and states that a violent thunderstorm will drop marble-sized hail pellets on your yard. Then the forecast shows you where all the hail will land and, incredibly, it predicts that the pellets will spell out 'Randal was right' on your back lawn."

With Sheridan still laughing, I plow ahead. "Sure enough, the following day everything happens just as predicted. Your guests amass underneath a big tent when the storm blows in and delivers an icy well-wish from above. Even though this event was predicted in advance in accord with known scientific laws, I have no problem saying that it's a lamp, given the meaningfulness of its signature. In fact, I think that would be a great example of God working within the supple laws of nature. This kind of action is surely something well within the ability of an omnipotent being."

Sheridan looks at me with admiration. "Okay, I'll admit that's pretty creative. In fact, you have a dangerously active imagination, Randal. It might be helpful if you dipped down into reality every once in a while."

"It doesn't matter how fanciful or implausible the story is. The lesson is the same. An event that's predicted in advance in accord with known scientific laws could carry a signature sufficiently suggestive that it's reasonable to conclude it was directed by an intelligence."

"Say a bit more about this idea of a 'signature' or 'sign' in events. It sounds pretty subjective to me. One person's mess is another person's message from God, right?"

"When complex, synchronous events occur, we only bother to invoke an intelligence if their occurrence makes sense within a context. If the hail had spelled out 'car' or 'bat' we would probably think it very unusual while not attributing to it any special significance. But 'Randal was right' is both highly complex and has a lot of significance—"

Sheridan interrupts me with a coughing fit that I choose to interpret as genuine. When he finishes, I continue.

"—and has significance to you, so you conclude that design is operative."

Sheridan squints at me skeptically.

"Okay," I say, "let's go back to hearing a song on the radio. Michael Jackson's song didn't have any significance to me at that moment, so I didn't feel compelled to draw any conclusions beyond coincidence. But it's easy to think of other cases where hearing a song on the radio would have special significance. Let's say that Buzz is trying to decide whether to enroll at Eastern University in his hometown of Philly or to go study at Westmont College in California. While praying for guidance he senses God telling him to turn on the radio. When he does, he hears the Village People singing 'Go West.' Given the background context, that's highly significant and would qualify as a lamp."

Sheridan looks incredulous. "Let me get this straight. You're recommending that good Christian kids choose their institutes of higher education based on whether they hear the Village People on the radio? What if 'In the Navy' happened to be playing instead? Should Buzz forgo college and join the armed forces?"

"Come on, it's an example. I'm just pointing out that if an event is highly complex and bears a suggestive signature pattern within the context . . . well, I think it's reasonable to view it as a divinely intended lamp. Buzz could certainly look for further corroborative evidence supporting this direction, but the song would at least provide some evidence."

"Okay, no more fanciful illustrations, Randal. How about moving on to some actual cases? What's a real lamp look like?"

"Let's start off with a modest lamp. I heard this one shared by William Lane Craig, a well-known Christian philosopher. Back in the 1980s, Craig began raising funds so he could serve as a missionary reaching European university students. After some time of intense fundraising he managed to raise all but three hundred dollars in the monthly pledges needed for support. Having canvassed all the churches and contacted all the donors he could find, Craig ran out of sources to cover the three-hundred-dollar shortfall. So he prayed about it. Then out of the blue he received a phone call from a man at one of the churches he had visited, calling to say that God had laid it on his heart to support Craig."

"Let me guess," Sheridan replies sarcastically. "He offered this Craig guy three hundred bucks, right?"

"That's right. Hey, have you been snooping in my notes?"

"You don't have to be a genius to see that one coming. Sorry to burst your bubble, Randal, but I've heard a million of those anecdotes at all the prayer meetings and revivals I was dragged to."

"It is true that there are a lot of 'friend of a friend' stories floating around. But I've heard Craig share his story and I take him to be a trustworthy testifier."

"Sure, whatever. I'm not saying he made it up. But is it such a stretch to think that it was just chance? Lots of things happen by chance that are even more unlikely than that. I mean, you're not seriously proposing that we should think Christianity is true because Craig needed three hundred bucks and someone gave it to him? What about all the times when Craig needed something and prayed and it didn't come? I bet he didn't count those."

"But why does it matter if Craig also had prayers that went unanswered? That doesn't change the fact that this prayer was answered."

"You're missing the point as usual, Randal. If most of Craig's prayers go unanswered, then he has a skewed selection sample. He's just choosing the prayers that get 'answered' as evidence for God. Once again you're just painting the target around the arrow. I'm sure you know that in double-blind scientific tests prayer has always failed to produce statistically significant results."

"Sorry, Sheridan, but I think you're the one missing the point. The Christian doesn't claim that prayer is directed at some abstract force that can be tested under laboratory conditions. This isn't a mere event cause at work that's constrained by a natural law. The claim, rather, is that God, an agent, answers prayer. And you can't stipulate how an agent is going to act. Still less can you do so when that agent is infinitely wiser than you because you simply cannot factor in all the knowledge that agent might consider in making his decision."

"Oh, yeah, of course, how convenient," Sheridan says with dripping sarcasm. "Believe me, if double-blind tests had vindicated prayer, you'd never give that reply. In that case you apologists would be trumpeting the power of prayer as vindicated by scientific laboratory tests."

"I wouldn't," I reply. "Remember how I said relationship matters most? Prayer isn't a magic spell to produce what we want every time. Listen, I introduced the Craig case as a relatively simple and modest instance of a lamp. But for the sake of argument let's fine-tune it further. Let's say Craig still needs to raise exactly $312.45, an amount unknown to anyone else. And lo and behold, a man calls him up and offers to give Craig $312.45. Would the specificity of that answer be enough for you to consider that God might be acting, even if Craig had all sorts of other prayers that were unanswered?"

"Nope."

"So what evidence would be sufficient for you? And by 'sufficient' I'm not asking what evidence would necessarily convert you to Christianity. I'm simply asking what would make you a bit more open to considering that there might be a divine being revealing himself through such signature events."

"I don't know. I'm pretty skeptical of all those anecdotes. As far as I'm concerned, you can always explain them as coincidence. There's no bigger 'chance event' than the evolution of life itself. After that, I'll chalk anything up to chance!"

"Okay," I say. "That's honest. But there is a danger in that kind of response."

"Which is?"

"My concern would be that invoking 'chance' or 'coincidence' can become a sweeping excuse to dismiss the evidential force of any event, no matter how compelling. Jesus knew this danger. In the parable of Lazarus and the rich man, the rich man suffering in Hades pleads that an angel be sent back to warn his brothers of his fate. Abraham responds, 'If they do not listen to Moses and the Prophets, they will not be convinced even if someone rises from the dead.'"[13]

"Well, that ain't true for me, Randal. If Jesus appeared before me right now I'd sit up and take notice. But I'm not going to start cooking a macaroni dish for the church potluck just because some dude I don't know received a check in the mail."

"That's an interesting admission. It seems to me very important to specify what kind of evidential lamps might have force for you, so I hope you don't mind if I explore this a bit."

Sheridan shrugs. "Go for it."

"A while ago I heard a discussion on the topic of miracles on a U.K. radio program called *Unbelievable*. One of the two guests was Adrian Holloway, a Christian apologist who argued that there are evidentially persuasive cases of miraculous healing. To back up his claim, he pointed to the case of a woman who was allegedly spontaneously healed of multiple sclerosis after a prayer meeting. Holloway was not relaying a mere anecdote. He stated he could provide a doctor's report confirming the details of the case. The other guest, well-known skeptic Michael Shermer, was surprisingly dismissive of Holloway's testimony. Instead of wanting to scrutinize the evidence of this particular claim, Shermer simply asked the general question of why God doesn't heal amputees as well."

"That's a fair question, isn't it?"

"Sure, so long as it isn't being raised as a red herring to avoid the evidence that a person was healed of MS. Interestingly, later in the interview Shermer admitted that he really wouldn't be persuaded of divine action even if an amputee spontaneously grew a limb following a prayer since this could possibly be a case of the body regenerating itself in a way we had not previously known to be possible!"

As Sheridan raises his eyebrows I quip, "Christian apologists aren't the only ones who love out-there thought experiments!"

I continue. "Think about it. Even if a pastor prayed, 'In Jesus' name, regenerate this limb!' and this prayer was followed by the limb growing back, Shermer still wouldn't consider that good evidence of divine action. That left me to conclude that for Shermer a natural explanation, no matter how implausible, is always the preferred one. Unfortunately, that's just a dogmatic and closedminded rejection of all possible lamps."

"It strikes me as pretty reasonable."

"Really?" I retort. "No matter how finely tuned the response to prayer might be? Don't you think that one should be more open to a more finely tuned signature? Granted a $300 answer to prayer may have relatively low complexity. But a $312.45 answered prayer would be significantly higher, and a $31,245.56 answered prayer would be very persuasive, I think. And what about an answered prayer for $312,455,600—"

"Okay, okay," interrupts Sheridan. "Perhaps. Maybe."

"That's an important concession because it means you can't just dismiss prayers that are answered in light of prayers that aren't. Even a single answered prayer that is sufficiently finely tuned can provide powerful evidence that God is in relation with us. The higher the specification of the answer, the more visible the signature—and the more likely that God is behind the event."

"The problem, Randal, is that I never hear examples that are from a credible source and that are of a sufficiently high level of complexity to persuade me. Every example I've heard can be explained by coincidence."

"Well, here's another example for you. Again, it's a contingent event that's complex and reveals a particular pattern. A student of mine named Lynn was going through a tough time with her family. Her husband was recovering from a heart attack and the whole family was feeling stressed out. Then her son came to her on Friday afternoon asking if the family could all go to the city's main water park for a break from the stress. Although it pained her, Lynn had to tell him that the water park was too expensive. Then about an hour later a knock came at the door. It was one of the members of their church who happened to have four extra passes to the water park and thought that Lynn and her family should have them."

Sheridan shakes his head in disdain. "Another Hallmark anecdote, huh?"

"Now hold on, Sheridan. I know Lynn. She didn't make that up. Don't be so quick to dismiss the signature in this event. The fact is that the tickets were offered within an hour of her son's request, and they weren't tickets to the zoo, the historical park or any of the many other attractions in the area: they were tickets to the water park. Four tickets. This was an event with a suggestive pattern that let Lynn know God was at work in her life. I'm not saying it's a perfect proof, but surely it has some evidential force. Even if there were other times when the wishes of Lynn's kids were not met, that shouldn't be an excuse for us to ignore the signature on this occasion."

"I'm sorry that I have to keep playing the rational skeptic, Randal. I feel like such a party pooper, but," Sheridan grabs my shoulder, "that is just a coincidence. Things like that happen all the time."

"William Temple had an interesting reply for you, Sheridan. He said, 'When I pray, coincidences happen, and when I don't, they don't.'"

Sheridan rubs his eyes in resignation. "Oh man, you just don't get it." He points toward a young Sikh man reading the newspaper at a nearby table. "You wanna bet whether that guy has his own stories of God's action in his life? Of course he does. So do Hindus and Muslims. Does that mean that all those religions are true, too?"

"That's not the way I'm using the cases, Sheridan. I'm not saying that different religions are true because people experience a corroboration of this type. I'm saying that if a person experiences lamps with a high degree of complexity and a suggestive signature pattern, then these events provide corroboration that God exists and that the person is relating to God from within his or her religious tradition.

That doesn't necessarily have any implications for the propositional truth of the religion in which the person participates."

Sheridan looks surprised. "So if that Sikh does have those same kinds of experiences, then you'd say that he was relating to God?"

"I couldn't negate the possibility a priori. I'd have to consider it on a case-by-case basis, I suppose. Let's say that a Sikh leader prays for a check to meet back payments for the mortgage on the gurdwara. They're in need of $34,342 to prevent the bank from taking possession, and nobody but the leader knows this. Suddenly a stranger knocks at his door with a check for that exact amount, explaining that Waheguru told him to write that exact amount."

"Who's Waheguru?"

"It's the Sikh name for God. That occurrence wouldn't necessarily make me think that Sikhism is true, but it would at least suggest that God is interested in meeting the needs of the local gurdwara. And that might increase my openness to considering whether God is at work in Sikhism."

Sheridan looks unsatisfied. "But do you count the ten thousand events in a day that don't have any pattern, or only the one event that does?"

"I thought I already addressed that point. But let's say that you and I are hiking on a trail and throughout the day we see thousands of rocks strewn on the path in a haphazard distribution. Then we come across about thirty rocks on the trail that are arranged to spell out, 'Hello hiker.' I say, 'Wow, looks like someone put those stones there to greet fellow hikers.' Would it make sense for you to respond, 'No way! In order to make that judgment you first need to consider all the thousands of rocks we saw today that didn't spell anything?' Sheridan, that'd be a crazy response. The haphazard distribution of the other rocks would have no significance for whether we ought to believe that these rocks were placed to provide a greeting, right?"

30

The Taliban and
the Serenity Prayer

* * *

O kay," Sheridan says with a tone of resignation, "I give up. Perhaps the experience of your 'lamps' provides some subjective confirmation to you Christians that you're in a saving relationship with God. Good for you. Really. I mean that. But that's still very far from the kind of confirmation of actual doctrines that I'd be looking for. How can you really know that all the claims of Christianity are true? The kinds of evidence that apologists provide—like the historicity of the resurrection or religious experience—that may be nice for you, since you're predisposed to believe it, but it seems to me to be a very slim reed on which to build a whole system of faith."

"First thing I want to stress, Sheridan, is that reasonable people can draw very different conclusions from the same data. If we want absolutely secure, irrefutable proofs that establish as true only one set of beliefs about reality, we are bound to be disappointed. All of us."

"And you're okay with that kind of ambiguity, Randal? Really? Look, I can live with two guys giving me conflicting directions to the same restaurant. I don't mind trying the one that seems more credible because if he's wrong I can still retrace my steps and try the other guy's directions. But we're talking about matters of supreme importance in which you only get one shot. You can't retrace your steps on this one after you die. Does God exist? If so, then who is he or she or it? And what does this God expect of us? You said that propositional knowledge about God is not as important as your knowledge of acquaintance. But there are many Christians who would disagree with you. Brother Mike believes you need to accept his church's doctrinal statement to be saved, and it's a big, long set of propositions. So why should I listen to you, some theology professor with your own agenda and baggage? Why shouldn't I listen to Mike with all his fundamental certainty? Hell, why not listen to some Taliban guy with the bomb strapped to his chest? After all, he's more certain than anybody! Let's say I decide to start following your directions. Maybe I make it to the destination. But maybe I don't. And then I find out after the fact that Mr. Taliban was actually right and Allah is completely raging at me. Or maybe Hinduism is right after all and for all my efforts I get reincarnated as a worm. What am I going to say on judgment day if I listen to you now and you're wrong? Can I say 'Yo, God, I was just following Randal's advice!' What if God says, 'Why'd you listen to that moron?'"

"That could happen, Sheridan. I could be wrong. We all could be. That's the human condition. Let me be clear: I'm not trying to 'close the deal' and make you convert to anything right now. All I'm asking is that you keep thinking about what you believe and whether it's an adequate view of the world—and whether you believe me or not, I'm asking myself those same questions all the time, too. I mean, if there is a God, he's an agent who is more than able to respond to honest prayers for guidance. We don't have to make any leaps of faith—we just keep taking reasonable steps and see where the road takes us. That's what I try to do."

"So you're not trying to save my soul today? That's a relief." Sheridan pauses and stares intently into the bottom of his empty coffee cup. "Mike treats doubt like a cancer. He wouldn't even consider you a Christian."

"Well, he wouldn't be the first," I reply. "I think we need to recognize the place of doubt and accept that it can also be a sign of spiritual health. Doubt forces us to keep thinking through our beliefs. I already gave you examples from my own experience. I have my doubts about divinely commanded genocide and eternal conscious torment. The proper response is not to run from those doubts, but rather to recognize them and wrestle with them."

Sheridan looks at me with a surprisingly pained expression. "But what do you do if you're wrong?"

"What can I do?" I reply. "You know the old 'Serenity Prayer' by Reinhold Niebuhr? 'God, grant me the serenity to accept the things I cannot change, courage to change the things I can, and wisdom to know the difference.'"

"Ick," Sheridan replies. "I think I've seen that on too many coffee mugs to take it seriously."

"I admit that it has been used a bit heavily in Christian kitsch. But even so I think it's still good advice. We can never attain a God's-eye point of view, so there's no benefit getting into an existential crisis about it. We just have to do our best with what we have, striving to know truth in all things and to be people of good character."

"Sounds okay with me. And until I see some evidence for God that convinces me, I'm going to keep sitting on the fence."

"Fine," I say. "Just don't fool yourself into thinking that sitting on the fence is a risk-free position. That's simply not the case. Not by a long shot."

"Oh really?" Sheridan sits up and looks interested. "Do tell."

"Okay, but are you ready for another thought experiment?"

Sheridan shrugs. "If only I had a lamp for every time you say that."

31

Feel Free to Sit on the Fence, but Don't Get Caught in the Lava Flow

★ ★ ★

Okay, imagine that you live in a small town on an island nestled in the shadow of a massive volcano. For several years there have been rumbles and shots of steam and ash as the volcano has continued to threaten an eruption. One day a visitor in a uniform with an identity card marking him as a government official announces in the marketplace that a massive eruption is imminent and that anyone who does not leave the island immediately will be killed by the blast. Unfortunately all the boats are out for a two-week fishing trip and the only way off the island is on this man's boat. The problem is that by leaving the island you effectively surrender your ownership of your land and house—thus leaving it to be claimed by any squatter who remains on the island.

"Clearly you've got to weigh your options carefully. If you leave the island and there is an eruption you'll save your life, but if you leave and there is no eruption, you'll lose your home. Conversely, if you stay and there is no eruption, then you're just fine, but if you stay and there is an eruption, then you lose your home and your life. This leaves you with a serious dilemma, Sheridan. Do you get on the boat or not?"

"I'd hold back on making a decision so that I could gather more information from the boat owner, run a background check on his credentials and get a second opinion from some volcanologists," Sheridan says.

"If you have the time," I reply. "But do you? Since this is my thought experiment, I'll tell you the answer: you don't. At present you're standing on the dock, smoke is curling up in growing plumes above the town, and the lineup to get on the boat is growing longer by the minute. You have to make a decision now. So what are you going to do?"

Sheridan is unimpressed. "This sounds exactly like the high-pressure evangelism sales tactics I grew up with: 'Do you know where you'd go if you died tonight?' You're just using fear to try to pressure me into making a commitment to Jesus."

"That's not my point, Sheridan. I want you to take me seriously when I say that I'm not trying to convert you at this instant. I'm telling you the volcano story for two reasons. The first is that volcanoes are awesome."

Sheridan's groan is audible.

"And the second," I continue, "is to point out that standing on the dock, or sitting on the fence, is not neutral. Whether you go forward, turn back or stay where you are, you are making a decision. That doesn't mean you need to let anyone pressure you into a new decision, but it does mean that it's wrong to think you can just 'sit on the sidelines' until you reach whatever level of certainty you're after. All of us are always in the game. Being a believer in anything brings risks with it, sure, but so does remaining a skeptic. We should be wary of the danger of doubt no less than of belief."

"Fine, but that doesn't change the fact that your beliefs are flimsy. Take the doctrine of the Trinity for instance. I take it that's a pretty important belief for Christians."

I nod. "Yup, it's at the core of Christian identity."

"Exactly. So how can you know that it's true? Maybe it's possible that there's a God. Maybe it's even more likely than not. But even with that concession you're still light years from confessing one God in three persons, aren't you? What kind of mental gymnastics do you have to do to make yourself believe that?"

"Sheridan, I don't disagree with apportioning your assent to the evidence. But that also means you can still believe those things for which the evidence is not as strong, but perhaps not with the same degree of conviction as some other things. For instance, a Christian could say that his belief in God is quite strong, but his belief that God is triune is less so."

"How can you be a Christian if you doubt the Trinity?"

"I didn't say a person would necessarily be doubting the Trinity. He could accept the proposition 'God is three persons.' He just wouldn't accept it with the same degree of certainty that he accepts some other propositions of the faith like 'God is the most perfect being' and 'God is love.' Remember that the Jews were in a covenantal relationship with God without ever believing that God is three persons. This means that at one point in history God revealed himself as one but not yet three. Christians believe that later revelation expanded and in some sense corrected the Israelites' belief. With that in mind, it would seem possible that in the future God might expand and correct Christian beliefs in similar respects. How can we know this isn't possible?"

Sheridan looks skeptical. "That sounds pretty wishy-washy to me. I'll make it simple for you: Do you believe in the Trinity?"

"Of course I do. But it's a big mistake to think you need to hold all Christian beliefs with the same level of conviction, as if it's 100 percent certainty or not at all. I believe the doctrine of the Trinity, but I could see myself being wrong on that. It's far more difficult to see myself being wrong on the existence of God. As for other doctrines, such as the nature and meaning of the Lord's Supper, I have even less conviction."

"Same thing with hell, I guess, right?"

"It's true that I'm not sure what to think about the doctrine of hell. I'm pretty sure that eternal conscious torment is not correct, though I could be wrong there, too. And if I am right, I'm not sure whether my present leanings toward annihilationism will be vindicated or whether my hope in the salvation of all might emerge triumphant. The point is that I can inhabit the Christian tradition, and even thrive within it, with all these remaining questions, doubts and qualifications. To my mind, this isn't being wishy-washy. It's recognizing the complexity of belief. The good news, Sheridan, is that we're not saved by how many beliefs we get right. We're saved by being in relationship with God."

"Right; your 'acquaintance knowledge.' But beliefs still matter, don't they?"

"Of course they matter, but salvation isn't a matter of simply getting a certain number of correct answers on a multiple choice exam. It's a complex process of moving into relationship with that being than which none greater can be conceived. And I believe that this being is the triune God who accomplished a redemptive work in Christ. That's the boat I chose to board."

"Well, I'm staying on the dock. I'm not deciding anything until all the evidence is in. And if I get buried in a lava flow, then so be it."

32

Adieu

Sheridan stands and stretches. "Listen, don't think your evangelistic pitch is scaring me off. I just need to get going. I must admit it's been interesting talking with you, Randal. It's also been interesting having a fly on the wall listening in the whole time."

He casts a glance your way and then looks back to me with a grin. "You don't suppose Reader minds being compared to a fly, do you?"

"Nah," I reply. "Reader's cool."

Looking out the window at the late-afternoon sunlight, Sheridan turns back to me. "I can't believe we've been debating all day."

It's true. The shadows are growing long in the Beatnik Bean as evening approaches. Talk about grande conversations! I stand to shake Sheridan's hand, a formality that catches him off-guard. "Thanks for hanging out, buddy," I say. "Maybe we'll do it again."

Sheridan nods noncommittally, grabs his backpack and then chuckles. "I admit, Randal, you're easier to take than most Christians I've met. But this whole day has been a bit weird: The fact that your crazy book bag has every possible prop, and Reader sitting there stone-silent the whole time. I dunno . . . it's like there's a *Truman Show* vibe going on."

"What do you mean?"

"Like I said, it's almost like our whole conversation was part of a book, like we were just characters in some story."

"You got it," I grin. "And you'll be famous. 'The Irish atheist agnostic in Randal Rauser's latest masterpiece!'"

As Sheridan makes his way to the door chuckling, I wave. "Adieu, Sheridan."

"Adieu?" Sheridan laughs as he walks out the entrance. "Now that's pompous! How about something a little less profound, like 'Smell ya later'?"

Without looking back, Sheridan gives a final wave and disappears into the twilight, a tinkling bell signaling his departure.

33

A Love Supreme

* * *

I sit back in the chair and look over at you.

"Well, Reader, what do you think?" I pause and study your solemn expression.

"You look a bit deflated," I say. "Wasn't what you expected? Don't lose sight of how far we've come. When Sheridan walked in that door, he thought belief in God was crazy and belief in the God of Christianity was simply off the charts, as arbitrary and indefensible as believing in Zeus or some other defunct deity. Now he's begun to recognize that religion's a lot more complex than that. No longer can he place himself on a pedestal of reason standing in judgment of all those committed to one religious perspective or another.

"Consequently, we've got him thinking through what he actually believes. He's going to have to get clear on whether he really is an atheist, an agnostic, a naturalist, a nihilist or something else. And whatever he decides he is, he knows he'll have to defend it. He's beginning to see that the 'skeptic' bears a burden of proof as surely as the believer.

"Plus, I think he's beginning to appreciate how signposts like goodness and meaning can be taken to point to a transcendent, personal foundation to the universe. And I think we've softened the objections he had to the God of Christian faith by expanding his options for thinking through biblical genocide and the doctrine of hell.

"After all, now he's seen that it's possible to live with doubt and to find the hand of providence in the little things. And we accomplished all this while being generally pleasant."

You look at me skeptically.

"Okay, more or less generally pleasant, some of the time," I add with a laugh. "Hopefully more rather than less. And that, I dare say, is more than can be said for some of the Christians in Sheridan's past like Mr. Benchley and 'Brother Mike.'

"And this was a real conversation, wasn't it? Sheridan challenged me several times. More than once I don't think I had the best answers for his questions. If I could do it over again, I'd probably say a few things differently. He certainly pushed me to keep thinking. The problem of evil, genocide, hell, prayer, religious pluralism and truth—these are all issues that I'm going to keep wrestling with. And that's okay. Remember, the conversation isn't about winning a debate. It's about moving toward the truth. And I dare say that we've all taken some steps in that direction today."

At that moment we hear the familiar sounds of John Coltrane's "Psalm" begin to play. The song rounds out "A Love Supreme," a monumental four-part suite of praise and thanksgiving to God. John intended that album to be a reverent offering to the God who had pursued him—and who pursues us all—while we were yet sinners.

I don't know if you'd call this a lamp or not, but as Trane's haunting saxophone slowly fills the coffee shop, somehow it seems just about right.

Acknowledgments

First I'd like to thank . . .

Volney James, publisher at Authentic/Biblica, who believed in the potential of one long apologetics conversation; my agent, Janet Kobobel Grant of Books and Such Literary Agency, who helped to make this conversation a reality; Rick Rauser, who read some of the chapters in draft form and offered some helpful comments; my editor at Biblica, David Jacobsen, whose eye for detail and offbeat humor resulted in a much improved book; InterVarsity Press for taking on this project late in the process and Al Hsu, associate editor at InterVarsity, for shepherding it through to completion; and finally the readers at my blog, "The Tentative Apologist" at http://randalrauser.com/blog/, especially those who take the time to post their own responses to my musings, the good, the bad and perhaps even the ugly. We may not all agree, but nobody said truth is easily discerned, so let's keep the conversations going.

Notes

[1] This is a central theme of my book *You're Not as Crazy as I Think: Dialogue in a World of Loud Voices and Hardened Opinions* (Colorado Springs: Biblica, 2011).

[2] John Loftus, "The Outsider Test for Faith Revisited," in *The Christian Delusion: Why Faith Fails,* ed. John Loftus (Amherst, N.Y.: Prometheus, 2010), p. 82.

[3] Lionel Nicholas, *Introduction to Psychology,* 2nd ed. (Cape Town, South Africa: UCT Press, 2008), pp. 102-3.

[4] Richard Dawkins, "Viruses of the Mind," in *A Devil's Chaplain: Reflections on Hope, Lies, Science and Love* (New York: Houghton Mifflin, 2003), p. 128.

[5] Colin McGinn, *Problems in Philosophy: The Limits of Inquiry* (Oxford: Blackwell, 1993), p. 98.

[6] *Oxford Companion to Philosophy,* ed. Ted Honderich (Oxford: Oxford University Press, 1995), p. 63.

[7] Fyodor Dostoyevsky, *The Brothers Karamazov,* trans. Ignat Avsey (Oxford: Oxford University Press, 2008), p. 793.

[8] Cited in Philip Carlo, *The Night Stalker* (New York: Pinnacle, 1996), p. 321.

[9] Ibid., p. 517.

[10] Werner Herzog, *Grizzly Man,* directed by Werner Herzog, written by Sujit R. Varma (Lions Gate Films, Discovery Docs, 2005), DVD.

[11] Friedrich Nietzsche, *The Gay Science,* trans. Walter Kaufmann (New York: Random House, 1974), p. 181.

[12] Psalm 34:8.

[13] Luke 16:31.